STUDIES IN ENGLISH LITERATURE

Volume CVII

10.5.77

ESSAYS ON CHAUCER'S SAINTS

by

ANN S. HASKELL

State University of New York at Buffalo

1976
MOUTON
THE HAGUE - PARIS

ISBN 90 279 3264 6

Printed in the Netherlands

TABLE OF CONTENTS

Preface vii
Introduction 1
1. The Host's precious corpus Madrian 7
2. The Pardoner's St. Ronyan. 17
3. The St. Giles Oath in the Canon's Yeoman's Tale 26
4. The St. Loy Oath Reconsidered 32
5. Hende Old St. Nicholas in the Miller's Tale. 38
6. St. Nicholas and the Prioress's Calendar 46
7. St. Nicholas and the Prioress's "cursed Jewes" 51
8. Attributes of Anger in the Summoner's Tale[St. Thomas] . 58
9. St. Simon in the Summoner's Tale 64
10. The St. Joce Oath in the Wife of Bath's Prologue 70
Bibliography 75

PREFACE

These essays were written over a long period of time. They were begun, in fact, in a graduate seminar in which I was enrolled at the University of Pennsylvania. They represent a variety of styles and reflect the changes that occur in individual scholarly perspective. While my approach would undoubtedly be somewhat different if I were considering the subject for the first time today, I have decided to let these essays stand for the most part as they were originally written.

Numerous kindnesses have been extended to me in the research and preparation of this book. I have received financial aid in the form of summer grants from the University Awards Committee of the State University of New York and research assistance from the State University of New York at Buffalo. As my research assistant, Dr. E. Carole Brown, now a faculty member of the State University College at Buffalo, was invaluable. And it is a special pleasure to record my appreciation of the generous amount of scholarly information and opinion given me by Margaretta Henry Soyez.

INTRODUCTION

This book might easily have been called The Picaresque Saint, if the
title had not been pre-empted by R. W. B Lewis for a group of essays
on a very different subject. Quite unwittingly he describes Chaucer's
holy man when he writes about "a very peculiar kind of saint, em-
bodying a peculiar sanctity, ... this figure - this strange, recurring,
half-hidden or wholly realized, sometimes antic, and in at least one
instance godless figure of sainthood. ... " 1* The following essays
deal with some of the saints - and one non-saint - used for special
effects in the Canterbury Tales.

Though these studies concern only the saintly allusions in the
Canterbury Tales, I am by no means suggesting that Chaucer con-
fined his saints' references to the Tales. The "Seynt Johan" oath in
the Book of the Duchess (BD 1318) illustrates this fact. The essays
do not deal with the purely factual, or "historical," saints, such as
the "hooly blisful martir" of the General Prologue or the ninety-
seven references to saints in the Parson's Tale. Rather, they concern the so-called "referential" saints, who, in one way or another,
subtly enhance their context. At the very least this enhancement is
double entendre; typically it is extended satire. The oath by St. Neot
(A 3771) in the Miller's Tale, for example, has the hallmarks of
an illuminating reference. Initially, it claims our attention because
it is sworn by a relatively unknown saint. His legend is fanciful and
is applied to an important part of what is probably Chaucer's most
popular tale. Because of the immediate context of the oath and because of the character to whom it is applied, we should expect something in the legend of St. Neot to expand the pithiness of the fabliau in
which it appears, either by comic compliment or ironic contrast.

We will not be concerned here with the historical accuracy of a
saint's vita, but rather with the legend which surrounds him. It is
our primary concern to determine what the mind of Chaucer's audience imagined when a given saint's name was mentioned. We are
concerned with the lore, regardless of how fabulous, that spun
around a name. The accretion of ideas from ecclesiastical art, myth,
confusion with other saints, breviaries, festivals and sermons are
all admissible as information. Northrop Frye's observation that
"in Cristianity the saints play a prominent role in absorbing local
gods" is perfectly true. 2* St. Nicholas is inextricably confused with
Poseidon, and St. Ronan, as we shall see, is hopelessly entangled
with the gods of pre-Christian nature worship.

Chaucer has used the names of saints in the Canterbury Tales in
much the same way as the medieval graphic artist used symbols in
depicting the saints' legends. That is, a single attribute - a flower,

an animal, or a tool - was used in a representation to suggest an entire incident in the saint's legend. Appearing most typically in oaths, the saints' names in the tales rapidly add depth to descriptions that would otherwise have required lengthy explanations to achieve the same effect. Since Chaucer's descriptive technique is the deft, economical Picasso-like sketch, the name with attached legend perfectly suited his purpose. Similarly, in the churches even the most 'lewed' of men could read entire legends of the saints with the aid of individualizing attributes. The whole fearsome story of St. Erasmus' martyrdom could be conjured up from the windlass shown in his hand. Never mind that his bowels wound around the instrument had once been only rope; the more horrendous the torture, the more wonderful was this Christianity! The story of St. Denis' decapitation was recalled by the head he always bore in his hands, and St. Uncumber's beard reminded men of her struggle to remain chaste. The breasts held by Agatha and the beehive of Ambrose were, likewise, symbols of their legends. The great cast of thousands in living stained glass excited minds dulled with dawn-to-dusk labor and lifetime residence within the confines of a few square miles.

The legends of the saints, far from stereotyped, represented a variety of genres. Under the protective banner of Christian didacticism, they acquainted those normally deprived of secular literature with elements of the fabliaux, the romances, and stories of the marvelous. As approved reading and viewing, these 'Arabian Nights of the Middle Ages' 3* were brought into the one place which guaranteed their widest circulation and perpetuation, the church. Even the isolated and the illiterate came to know the saints from carved wood and sculpted stone, from sermons and from the church attendance which was compulsory on the numerous saints' festivals throughout the liturgical year.

With such a universally-recognized body of material as saints' lore at his disposal, it is hardly surprising that Chaucer drew on that common knowledge for quick response from his audience. While we must now struggle to understand some of Chaucer's saintly references, they were readily perceived by fourteenth century listeners. The wit of the few that we do comprehend makes the effort of further investigation worthwhile. The saints' references are pungent allusions which can color entire passages or quite alter our impressions of single characters. Though quick thrusts, the allusions are characterized by depth. It is significant that they attach themselves to the royalty of the Canterbury Tales, such as the Wife of Bath, the Pardoner and the Host, pilgrims who are most admired for their reality. As highly distilled metaphor, hagiographical allusions often appear in the most compressed passages. It is important that they introduce; they are found typically in prologues, where Chaucer strives for succinctness. And the saint is often used for Chaucerian irony. An incongruous saint can throw an entire passage in which it is embedded into vivid relief against it. An instance of tightly worked irony is the short passage at the beginning of the Monk's Prologue (B^2 3079-3113) in which the saint (Adrian) and his symbols, scattered throughout the material, contrast sharply with the surface action of the poetry. Similarly, the impression of the courtly Prioress, informed by the St. Loy oath in the General Prologue (A 120), carries over to her tale, where it interacts with several facets of St. Nicholas' legend.

While the saints were outranked by many other members of the army of the blessed, their relationship with medieval man was a much more personal one than that of, say, the Holy Trinity. The angels, God, Christ were regarded with awe. A saint, however, having formerly been a human peer, understood human needs and frailties. The saints were valued friends at court. 4* Their afflictions were those of the flesh - St. Appolonia's omnipresent toothache and St. Erasmus' perpetual bellyache - and they were beseeched according to the particular bailiwick of misery over which they presided. St. Christopher aided the traveler, St. Nicholas the child, St. Giles the cripple. St. Roch protected against both fire and plague and Lucy was invoked for eye diseases. If one were a prisoner he remembered Nicholas, and if he imprisoned others he thought on Adrian. The saints were not only invoked for deliverance from disaster, but in a preventive capacity as well. Each of the trades had its patron saint and there were specific occasions in the year set aside for homage of the guilds to their chosen saints. And cities, countries and villages each claimed saintly protectors who were duly honored also.

While the vehicle for the saintly allusion is frequently the oath, saints as characters (Nicholas, Godelieve), and simple references to saints (B^2 1704) are also used. Although the actual name of the saint usually appears only once, it is frequently accompanied by several of the symbols associated with it, forming a traditional icon. These icons are presented in the literary pictorialism of Jean Hagstrum and, more recently, John B. Bender 5*, and may appear straightforwardly or "up-so-doun," as in the Summoner's Tale, where Chaucer has used an iconic inversion at either end. 6*

In addition to expanding descriptions, the saint's reference may also be employed in word-play. Paronomasia such as the juxtaposition of (St.) Ronan with runian 'farmhand, scab, testicle' in the Pardoner's headlink is an example. Further investigation might easily reveal additional word-japes of this variety. Despite the disclaimers of earlier Chaucerians that their man would not stoop to such literary baseness, puns in the Canterbury Tales continue to be brought to light. 7* For example, the Miller's piping the pilgrims "out of towne" (A 566) puns on 'town': 'tune', and the Summoner's Tale shows possibilities of puns in several lines. Word-play such as that in the story of Pedro of Spain (Monk's Tale, B^2 3576), with its "wikked nest" translation of mau ni as a play on the name of Sir Oliver Mauny, suggests what further probing may reveal. That the saints' legends and patronages are also prone to twists, puns and the like, heightens the possibility of finding such word-play in the Chaucerian saints' references. St. Olaf (Holofius) is the patron saint of bakers, who have mistaken his name for "whole loaf," and the vin in St. Vincent's name has earned him the patronage of the wine industry.

The collection of essays that follows is not to be construed as comprehensive; it represents only a part of the total number of saints Chaucer included in the <u>Canterbury Tales</u>. It is, rather, representative of the many different ways in which the saintly references can inform their containing tales. These studies also suggest the variety of approaches which must be used to investigate the different referential saints. No two saints or their contexts are alike and each demands an individual method of study.

The geographical coensiveness of Chaucer's saints is rather remarkable, as the following map shows. The coasts of Brittany and Normandy accommodate most of the local saints, as well as showing special interests (centers of cults, and the like) of the universally popular ones such as Adrian. This area coincides with a geographical region Chaucer knew well, 8* implying firsthand knowledge of shrines, pilgrimages and folklore.

Though the saints do provide a way in to Chaucer, they constitute a key, not the key to the <u>Canterbury Tales</u>. Like some Joyce scholars, a few Chaucerians believe that they need only to find the right spot in their literary fish to plunge in the fillet knife and - <u>voila</u>! - they can lift out the bones intact. The <u>Tales</u> are not, however, arranged around any one central skeleton, be it the seven sins, marriage modes, attitudes toward Christianity or medieval rhetoric. An encyclopedic classic, they incorporate all of these approaches and will probably accommodate future literary fancies still te be conceived.

NOTES

1* R. W. B. Lewis, <u>The Picaresque Saint</u> (Philadelphia/New York, 1959), p. 31.
2* Northrop Frye, "Literature and Myth, " <u>Relations of Literary Study</u> (New York, 1967), pp. 32-33.
3* Helen C. White, <u>Tudor Books of Saints and Martyrs</u> (Madison, 1963), p. 29.
4* R. L. P. Milburn, <u>Saints and Their Emblems in English Churches</u> (Oxford, 1961), p. xv.
5* Jean Hagstrum, <u>The Sister Arts</u> (Chicago, 1958); John B. Bender, "A Theory of Literary Pictorialism, " presented to the General Topics 9 (Literature and Other Arts) Group, MLA, December, 1968, and see also Bender's discussion of Chaucer in <u>Spenser and Literary Pictorialism</u>, forthcoming by Princeton University Press, 1972.
6* John V. Fleming, "The Summ ner's Prologue: An Iconographic Adjustment, " <u>Chaucer Review</u>, (1967), 95-107, and see Chapter 8, on St. Thomas, which follows.
7* For example, Paull F. Baum's "Chaucer's Puns, " <u>PMLA</u>, LXXI (1956), 225-246, and "Chaucer's Puns: A Supplementary List, " <u>PMLA</u>, LXXIII (1958), 167-170; Helge Kökeritz, "Rhetorical Word-Play in Chaucer, " <u>PMLA</u>, LXIX (1954), 937-952; Norman D. Hinton, "More Puns in Chaucer, " <u>American Notes and Queries</u>, II (1964), 115-116.
8* Maurice Hussey, <u>Chaucer's World: A pictorial Companion</u> (Cambridge, England, 1967), p. 12, Inset 'B. '

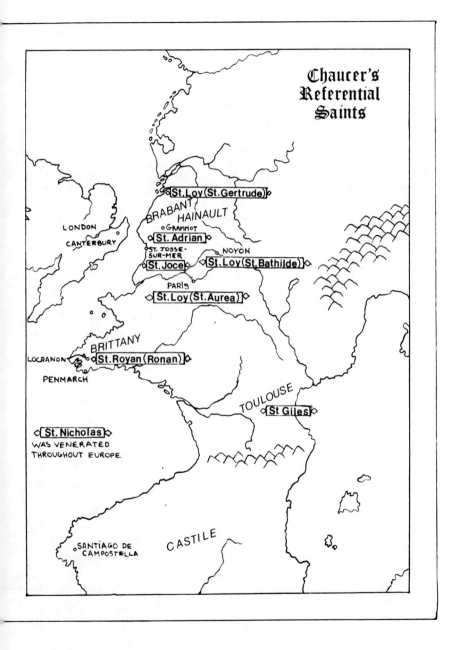

Chaucer's Referential Saints

St.Loy(St.Gertrude)

BRABANT HAINAULT

LONDON

CANTERBURY

o GRAMMOT

St. Adrian

ST. JOSSE-SUR-MER

St. Joce

NOYON

St.Loy(St.Bathilde)

PARIS

St.Loy(St.Aurea)

BRITTANY

LOCRANON

St.Royan(Ronan)

PENMARCH

TOULOUSE

St Giles

St. Nicholas

WAS VENERATED THROUGHOUT EUROPE

o SANTIAGO DE CAMPOSTELLA

CASTILE

Veneration of the referential saints in the <u>Canterbury Tales</u>

1

THE HOST'S Precious corpus Madrian*

The identity of Madrian, by whose precious corpus Harry Baily
swears in the Monk's Prologue (B^2 1892), has intrigued several
scholars. 1* Since Harry swears by his Christianity - "as I am feith-
ful man" - and since most oaths involve holy men, Madrian is probably a saint, an ecclesiastic whose body is important in his legend.
A candidate saint's name should agree as closely as possible with
the one in B^2 1892, and he must have been known to Chaucer's audience. Though there are instances of oaths in the Canterbury Tales
which are sworn by saints of immense popularity, such as Thomas
à Becket (A 3291, 3425, 3461, etc.), which can be taken at face
value, the use of a name even relatively unusual implies a special
relationship between saint and context, as with the Prioress and
St. Loy.
    There are several saints whose names bear a resemblance to
Madrian: Madron (Madern, Matronus), a sixth century Cornish saint;
Mathurin (Maturinus), a fourth century French saint, included in
the Golden Legend, whose precious body is mentioned in his story;
Materne (Maternus), a fourth century saint, bishop of Cologne and
possibly of Trier; Modan, a sixth century abbot, linked by tradition
to the abbey of Dryburgh; Matrona, the name of three early women
martyrs, one of Salonika, one of Barcelona and one of Capua; 2*
and Madryn, a sixth century English abbess, granddaughter of
Vortigern. 3* Of all these saints, only the legend of Mathurin mentions a body prominently, but neither he nor any of the rest of the
list attained widespread prominence. The cultus of Mathurin was
restricted to Sens.
    Dorothy M. Norris, having considered and rejected most of the
above-mentioned saints for B^2 1892, suggested that madrian was not
the name of a saint at all, but of a wine. 4* Subsequently G. L. Frost
reported the medieval use of the word madrian 'confection.'5*
Neither these two suggestions, nor any of the earlier identifications
of Madrian as a saint, however, is strikingly appropriate: the
precious corpus is not explained. It seems significant that no recent
edition of the Canterbury Tales gives a definite identification of
Madrian. 6*
    There is one variant of Madrian, involving the least possible
change of the name, which has not been considered; thus far, Adrian
has been overlooked. This name does appear as a manuscript variant.
It is found as both Adrian and Adryan. 7*
    There have been a number of saints named Adrian. 8* Of those known
in western Europe, few attained prominence beyond their own lo--

*This chapter was published originally in the Journal of English and
Germanic Philology, LXVII (1968), 430-440.

calities. Among the three Adrians who were known in England, a distinction is fairly well maintained. Pope Adrian III (A.D. 885), who is consistently identified by his title, cannot, therefore be considered for B² 1892. Abbot Adrian of St. Augustine's, Canterbury (A.D. 709) is usually identified not only by his title but with the place designation as well. He, too, must be ruled out as a candidate for B² 1892: while the tomb of Adrian of Canterbury attracted pilgrims (many of whom had probably come to visit the nearby shrine of St. Thomas à Becket), and while this saint was considered responsible for miraculous cures, the body itself was interred for causes of natural death. 9*

The most prominent among the saints named Adrian is a late third centiry Greek martyr, whose legend is not only given lengthy treatment in the Golden Legend, 10* but is well preserved in numerous documents of both east and west, such as the Roman Martyrology and the Martyrology of Jerome. 11* The salient features of the story are as follows:

> Adrian of Nicomedia was an officer at the imperial court during the Christian persecutions, probably under Diocletion. He was converted to the faith by the example of his prisoners and by his Christian wife, Natalia. He remained steadfast in his belief throughout imprisonment, agonizing torture and eventual death caused by the crushing and subsequent severing of his limbs on an anvil. He was martyred c. 290 A.D. and his wife, St. Natalia, who is also considered a martyr since she sustained and encouraged him throughout his ordeal, 12* died a short time afterwards.

There are many variations and miracles attached to this basic legend.

The longevity of St. Adrian's recognition is noteworthy. His name appears in two epitaphs attributed to Pope Damasus (366-384 A.D.). 13* 13* During the seventh century Pope Honorius (625-640 A.D.) converted the old Roman Senate House, the Curia Senatus on the Forum, into the Church of San Adriano, in honor of St. Adrian. 14* An early record of St. Adrian in England appears in the Old English Martyrology, 15* a ninth century translation of an unidentified Latin manuscript. 16* Another record of the saint which has particular relevance to English Literature is found in an itinerary of William of Malmesbury's twelfth century Gesta regum anglorum, in an account of the Crusade under Pore Urban II. Malmesbury inserted in the Gesta an early account, the Notitia Portarum Viarum Ecclesiarum circa urbem Roman, "one of the most reiable of the itineraries, " which has been dated from between 649 to the early eighth century. 17* Perhaps of greatest significance to the fourteenth century, however, is the saint's inclusion in not only a majority of rituals in England, 18* but specifically in the Sarum Use, the most widespread rite in England until the Reformation. 19*

The dates of celebration for St. Adrian have been several. 20* His martyrdom occurred on March 4, the date under which he is listed in the Old English Martyrology. By far the most important of his feast days, however, has been the date of his translation to Rome, September 8. To this date is probably attributable Adrian's longevity

in the Christian calendar, inasmuch as it is also the important
Marian feast, the Nativity of the Blessed Virgin. The present-day
Roman Catholic Daily Missal, in which St. Adrian is still included,
explains the connection of the saint with this particular date: "The
liturgy of our Lady's Birthday in Rome included a procession which
set out from the Church of St. Adrian in the forum. From this arose
the custom of commemorating St. Adrian on September 8 in connection with today's feast." 21* This association between the Nativity
and St. Adrian must have already been established by the close of
the seventh century. The life of Sergius I (687-701 A. D.) includes
a statement that this pope "directed that on the Annunciation, Nativity, and Assumption of our Lady, and in the festival which the Greeks
call Hypatante, a procession (litania) should go from St. Adrian's
to St. Mary Major's." 22*

The importance in England of September 8, primarily as the Nativity of the Blessed Virgin, and secondarily as the feast of St. Adrian,
is noteworthy. In addition to regular inclusion in lists of compulsory
observances of the church, September 8 was significant for other
reasons. Knowles notes "an interesting passage in the Abingdon
chronicle which records that all those connected with the brethren
who came to the monastery on the vigil of the Nativity of Our Lady
(8 September) were given hospitality." 23* The importance of the
occasion in early Chester can be seen in that it was one of the seven
special days of the year, in addition to the twelve days after Christmas
and the Sabbath, on which fines for bloodshed were increased from
ten to twenty shillings. 24* The Nativity was especially important at
Lichfield. In Richard II's Gild Ordinances of 1387 is recorded the
fact that the town's Gild of St. Mary held its annual account day and
feast on that date. 25* Of more widespread appeal, however, was
the riding of the bounds of Lichfield on the Nativity of the Blessed
Virgin. The so-called Sheriff's Ride, an annual affair lasting all
day, included many stops for refreshment and general festivity along
the route of the officials of the town. Though the extant ordinance
requiring the ceremony is recorded in 1553, 26* the custom of
beating, riding, or perambulating the bounds, the genesis of which
can be traced to the fifth century in Britain, 27* was probably in
force in Lichfield long before the sixteenth century. Wherever
celebrated, the occasion was one in which ale-gifts were bestowed,
and in Worcester, for example, even the prisoners in the County
Gaol were remembered with bequests "wherewith" to forget their
sorrows for a time, "presumably by indulging in what was called in
those times, "a heavy wet." " 28* It is quite possible, then, that St.
Adrian, by traditional connection with riding the bounds on the Nativity of the Virgin at Lichfield, received some sort of recognition: in
the margin of the Old English Martyrology manuscript, beside the
legend of St. Adrian, there is a drawing of a church, under which is
the word lechfelde. 29*

Perhaps the most important factor in Adrian's candidacy for VII
1892 is the disposal of his precious corpus. Not only was the muti-
lation of Adrian's body extreme and memorable, but the distribution
of it after death is truly remarkable. In a delightfully meiotic state-

ment, Baring-Gould says that "these relics have undergone par-
tition." 30* The first separation of bones occurred when St. Natalia
secretly took one of the saint's severed hands after his death, although she is supposed to have returned it to the rest of the body
when the Christians obtained possession of the corpse of Adrian to
bury it at Argyropolis, near Byzantium. After death, but before
burial, Adrian's body is reputed to have appeared to the pilot of a
ship on which Natalia was being abducted with other Christians,
giving advice for their safety. Natalia died and was buried beside
her husband a short time thereafter. Subsequently the bodies were
translated to Rome, where the bones of Adrian, at least, were
reported to have been buried under the high altar of the Church of
San Adriano. Both Adrian and Natalia are thought to have been translated to the Abbey of S. Pedro de Estonça in the ninth century. The
arms of both are reputed to be at Leon in the monastic church of
S. Claudius and another portion at Bolneare, near Leon. Relics of
these saints are reported at Chellas, near Lisbon, and still others
are listed as being in the reliquary in an abbey which is dedicated to
them near Ovideo. Adrian's jaw and half an arm are at Cologne,
while another fragment of an arm bone is claimed at Prague. 31*
The list of relics at Salisbury Cathedral also shows "A relike of
Seint Adryan" 32* and the Canterbury inventories include "some
bones of St. Adrian, martyr." 33* Further, there are two teeth at
St. Crepin in Hainault, part of an arm at Floreffe, an arm at Lobbes,
and another tooth at Ninove in Flanders. There are claims of some
bones of St. Adrian at Agincourt, Douai, as well as Bruges in the
Cathedral and at the Jesuit church at Mecheln. An entire body of the
saint is thought to rest in Ghent and his head is supposedly at Bolog-
na. Of all the relics, however, the most renowned are those at
Grammont Geraardsberg), a town near the Hainault border. This
means that there are claims of at least three whole bodies of the
saint in or near Belgium. 34*

The veneration of St. Adrian at Grammont, only twenty miles
southeast of Ghent, would surely have been familiar to the English
royal family. Chaucer's queen, Philippa, was of course, a native
of Hainault, as was his wife Philippa. Considering the emphasis on
Adrian in Flanders, the saint may well have had special significance
for the royal family. The records of Grammont abbey show that
among distinguished visitors to the shrine of St. Adrian was the
"ducissa Lancastriae" in 1376. 35* (Lancaster was in Flanders from
October, 1375 to March 12, 1376. 36*) This visit by John of Gaunt's
wife would probably have included Philippa Chaucer in the retinue as
well. Constance may also have made a 1374 trip to Grammont:
Froissart reports that Gaunt's son, also John of Gaunt, who did not
live to adulthood, was born on the return of the Duchess of Lancaster
from a pilgrimage to Saint Adrien de Grammont. 37* The distribution
of Adrian's relics in Spain as well as Flanders, suggests the saint's
popularity in both places. Lancaster, as Constance's husband, was
titular King of Spain, in addition to his English, French and Flemish
power. There is also a "conjecture that the Sarum use was followed
in the diocese of Lisbon from shortly after the capture of the city in

1147 until 1536. . . ." 38* There is further suggestion of the saint's popularity in the royal family. Among the relics owned by Edward II, to whom Philippa was queen, was a "chest of wood covered with cloth in which [were] two crystal vessels enclosed in silver gilt, . . . [in one of which was contained] a tooth of St. Adrian." 39*

St. Adrian would have been familiar to the general English public of the fourteenth century, as well as to the nobility. In addition to his inclusion in the Sarum ritual, by which every churchgoer would have been reminded of him at least annually, he was the patron saint of brewers, both English 40* and Flemish. 41* The importance of this trade in Chaucer's time can hardly be over-stated. Pendrill, commenting on the "universality of beer as the popular beverage at a time when tea, coffee, and cocoa were unknown," estimates that in the latter fourteenth century there was "one drink shop to every twelve inhabitants." 42* In 1309, according to the Liber Albus, there were 354 taverns and 1334 brewers in London. 43* The brew was far weaker then than now 44* and, inasmuch as the tavern constituted one of the only real places for congregation outside the church, as well as a place of business transaction, great quantities of beer and ale must have been consumed. 45*

F. W. Hackwood is puzzled by the choice of St. Adrian as the patron of the brewing trade. 46* It is probably due, however, to the saint's association with the Nativity of the Blessed Virgin Mary. In the south of France on the Ascension of Mary, August 15, and in the north on the Nativity of Mary, September 8, the harvesting of crops was begun. The first products of these harvests, especially the grapes and grains, the raw materials of wine, ale and beer, were brought to Mary as an offering. The occasion was an important one, with many local variations, such as the driving down of cattle from their mountain pastures in Switzerland. Whatever the local customs, however, there was traditionally much celebration on this occasion, and the coincidental commemoration of St. Adrian on the same date made him an appropriate patron of the drink which undoubtedly flowed copiously on his feast day. 47*

Adrian was also the patron saint of jailers and executioners, chosen by them to protect their victims, since he had survived imprisonment and triumphed over death. The blacksmiths chose him as a patron because the instrument of his martyrdom was the anvil. Messengers adopted Adrian as their saint because he brought messages to his wife in two appearances after his death. And he was the patron saint of butchers, as well. 48*

Adrian was invoked against meningitis in Normandy and sudden death and plague elsewhere. Mâle notes that "Sts. Sebastian, Adrian and, from the fourteenth century, Roch were the protectors of towns against the plague." 49* His invocation in this capacity in Amiens, where he was greatly revered, is especially important. 50* Adrian's triumph over an epidemic of pestilence in Lisbon earned him a niche as a patron of that city. 51* His most important patronage, however, was that of soldiers. "Adrian was long considered in northern Europe as the chief military saint next to St. George. [He] was, in Flanders and Germany and the north of France, what Sebastian was in Italy. "52*

One story of Adrian reports that Emperor Henry II, St. Henry, when about to begin an expedition against the Turks and Hungarians, buckled on St. Adrian's sword, preserved at Walbeck, in Saxony, as a precious relic. 53*

The terrible physical violation of St. Adrian, among the most atrocious of tortures in all Christian martyrdom, made his legend an especially attractive one among the "religious Arabian nights." 54* He has been the subject of many works of art over the centuries and was well represented in the fourteenth. He was identifiable by his symbol, the anvil, and was garbed as a warrior saint in armour. In addition to the anvil, he is sometimes depicted with severed arms and legs, as well. And not infrequently St. Natalia is shown at Adrian's side. Though the saint is very well represented on the continent, little of his iconography survives in England. A roodscreen at Stoke Poges is extant, and another may be seen at Walborough in Devon. 55* Heavy losses in medieval English wall-painting and other media of ecclesiastical art, such as stained glass, from natural deterioration and destruction at the Reformation probably account for missing representations of St. Adrian. 56* Further, confusion among saints whose symbols or garb was similar was not infrequent. 57*

Miscellaneous references to St. Adrian may be found in other English sources. He is included in a list of saints mentioned in the parish churches of East Kent, at both Ashford and at Boughton Malhere. While Adrian of Canterbury might be suspected in Kent, the saint's name is followed by "March 4," one of St. Adrian of Nicomedia's feast days, 58* and reference is made to "Abbot Adrian of St. Augustine's" elsewhere in the same series. 59*

The legend of St. Adrian is especially appropriate to the Monk's Prologue; there are several possible echoes of the story in the first thirty-four lines of "the murye wordes of the Hoost." In the line immediately following the Madrian oath, for example, Harry Baily's desire that his wife hear the Tale of Melibee, exceeds even that for 'a barel ale.' That St. Adrian was the patron saint of brewers makes the expression especially pithy. The lines in which Harry bemoans Goodelief's demands for worldly recognition (B^2 1901 f.), are in contrast with Natalia's:

"You are blessed, Adrian, for you have found the riches which your father and mother did not leave to you, and which the wealthy themselves have need of in the day when neither father nor mother nor children nor friends nor earthly goods are of any avail." 60*

In B^2 1906-1907 the Host's wife, belittling Harry, declares sarcastically "I wol have thy knyf, / And thou shalt have my distaf and go spynne!" The wife's assumption of the male role, though for quite a different reason, is found in the legend of Adrian and Natalia also: in order to be admitted to her husband's prison, Natalia not only dresses herself as a man, but even crops her hair. 61* (Spinning is the only domestic activity of Goodelief or Natalia that is ever mentioned in connection with either woman.)

Another possible reference to the Adrian legend is found in the reported complaint of the Host's wife (B^2 1306-1307): " 'Alas!' she seith, 'that evere I was shape/ To wedden a milksop, or a coward ape.' " This may be compared to a lament by Natalia, made when she believes Adrian to have recanted his Christianity: "Helas! malheureuse que je suis! que ferai-je, moi qui suis unie a un homme de la race des perfides?" 62*

One more possible connection between the vita of Sts. Adrian and Natalia and the Monk's Prologue is found in B^2 1916 in the reference to a lion. Both of these saints are often depicted with a lion lying at their feet. The beast found in the representations of the saints is the lion of fortitude, which has strong associations with the heraldic lions of Belgium. Like a medieval graphic artist's placement of a symbol at the bottom of a picture, Chaucer's short domestic sketch of Harry Baily and his wife is also completed with a lion. But Harry's comparison to a lion hardly suggests fortitude. Chaucer has him complain that in order to please his shrewish wife he must "Be lik a wilde leoun, fool-hardy." In this instance and, indeed, in the entire passage, a reading in comparison with the legend of St. Adrian reveals a satirically rich substratem.

NOTES

1* See The Works of Geoffrey Chaucer, ed. W. W. Skeat, 2nd ed. (London, 1900), V, 224, for early scholarship.
2* See Alban Butler, Lives of the Saints, eds. Herbert Thurston, S. J. and Donald Attwater, 4 vols. (New York, 1956); Sabine Baring-Gould, Lives of the Saints, 2nd ed., 13 vols. (London, 1897); The Book of Saints, Benedictine Monks, St. Augustine's Abbey, Ramsgate, 4th ed. (New York, 1947); F. G. Holweck, A Biographical Dictionary of the Saints (London, St. Louis, 1924).
3* Holweck, pp. 636-637.
4* Dorothy Norris, "Harry Bailey's 'Corpus Madrian,' " MLN, XLVIII (1933), 146-148.
5* George L. Frost, "That Precious Corpus Madrian," MLN, LVII (1942), 177-179.
6* See, for examples: The Works of Geoffrey Chaucer, ed. F. N. Robinson, 2nd ed. (Cambridge, Mass., 1957), p. 745; Chaucer's Poetry, ed. E. T. Donaldson (New York, 1958), p. 360; Chaucer's Major Poetry, ed. A. C. Baugh (New York, 1963), p. 353; Selections from the Tales of Canterbury, ed. R. A. Pratt (Boston, 1966), p. 170. Jp John R. Byers, Jr., in a short article in 1966 has also suggested St. Adrian ("Harry Bailey's St. Madrian," English Language Notes, IV, 6-9). Through the vagaries of scholarly publishing, my work on this subject, completed in 1966, is published originally under the date of 1968. Byers has explained the addition of the initial M to Adrian through wrong division between the saint's name and the Latin ending of the preceding word.
7* John M. Manly and Edith Rickert, The Text of the Canterbury Tales (Chicago, 1940), III, 464.
8* See n. 2, supra.

9* Baring-Gould, I, 128-131.

10* Jacques de Voragine, La Légende Dorée (Paris, 1843), I, 374-379.

11* Acta Sanctorum [AASS], Vol. III for September, 209-255. See also bibliographies in: Butler's Lives, III, 507-508; Bibliotheca Sanctorum, Pontificia università Lateranense (Rome, 1961), pp. 270-271.

12* Lucy Menzies, The Saints in Italy (London, 1924), p. 3: "Natalie is a martyr because ... she endured greater anguish by witnessing her husband's pain. " See also Helen C. White, Tudor Book of Saints and Martyrs (Madison, 1963), p. 4 and her reference to Edelhard L. Hummel, The Concept of Martyrdom according to St. Cyprian of Carthage (Washington, D. C. , 1946).

13* Ethel R. Barker, Rome of the Pilgrims and Martyrs (London, 1912), p. 304.

14* Fernand Gregoronius, History of the City of Rome in the Middle Ages, trans. Annie Hamilton, 4th ed. (London, 1884), pp. 121-122.

15* Ed. George Herzfeld, Early English Text Society, no. 116 (London, 1900), pp. 32-34.

16* Stanley B. Greenfield, A Critical History of Old English Literature (New York, 1965), p. 41.

17* Barker, pp. 117-118.

18* See the Henry Bradshaw Society series, for example, St. Adrian, martyr, celebrated 8 Sept. in 7 of 11 litanies in English Benedictine Kalendars after A. D. 1100 (London, 1934), Vol. I; The Martiloge, eds. Francis Proctor and E. S. Dewick (London, 1893), p. 36.

19* Breviarium Ad Usum Insignis Ecclesiae Sarum, edd. Francis Proctor and Christopher Wordsworth, I (Canterbury, 1882), A3, Kalendar for March; Oxford Dictionary of the Christian Church, ed. F. L. Cross (London, 1957), v., Sarum; Archdale A. King, Liturgies of the Past (Milwaukee, 1958), p. 277.

20* See AASS, loc. cit. ; Holweck, 19-20; Walter H. Frere, The Kalendar: Studies in Early Roman Liturgy (London, 1930), I, 131.

21* Daily Missal, v. Sept. 8.

22* K. A. Heinrich Kellner, Heortology (London, 1908), p. 229.

23* M. D. Knowles, The Monastic Orders, 2nd ed. (Cambridge, Eng. , 1963), p. 481: Chron. Abingd. , II, 313.

24* "English Towns and Gilds, " ed. Edward P. Cheyney, Translations and Reprints from the Original Sources of European History, II (Philadelphia, 1895), 3.

25* The Gild of St. Mary Lichfield, ed. F. J. Furnivall, EETS 114 (London, 1920), pp. 4-5.

26* Dorothy G. Spicer, Yearbook of English Festivals (New York, 1954), p. 126.

27* A. R. Wright, British Calendar Customs, Publications of the Folk-Lore Society (London/Glasgow, 1940), III, 63-64, 68; I, 129-137.

28* Ibid. , I, 136.

29* Herzfeld, p. 32.

30* Baring-Gould, I, 117.

31* Ibid. , 118.

32* Ceremonies and Processions of the Cathedral Church of Salisbury, ed. C. Wordsworth (Cambridge, 1901), p. 36.

33* J. Charles Wall, Shrines of British Saints (London, 1905), p. 15:
St. Adrian, Martyr, is here (p. 15) distinguished from "St. Adrian,
the abbot who accompanied St. Theodore to England" (p. 22).
34* Baring-Gould, I, 117-118; see also Holweck, loc. cit. ; J. Corblet,
Hagiographie du diocese d'Amiens, IV (Paris/Amiens, 1874), 129-130;
Louis Réau, Iconographie de L'art Chrétien, III, pt. 1 (Paris, 1958),
23-24; Karl Künstle, Ikonographie der heiligen (Freiburg-im-Breisgau, 1926), 31-32.
35* AASS, Sept. , III, 239.
36* Sydney Armitage-Smith, John of Gaunt (New York/London,
1905), p. 119, n. 1.
37* Oeuvres de Froissart, ed. Kervyn de Lettenhove, III (Brussels,
1869), 467.
38* King, pp. 284-285.
39* Edith Rickert, Chaucer's World, edd. C. C. Olson and M. M. Crow
(New York/London, 1948), p. 390.
40* F. W. Hackwood, Inns, Ales and Drinking Customs of Old England
(New York, n. d.), p. 81.
41* The Reader's Encyclopedia, ed. William Rose Benét (New York,
1955), p. 966.
42* Charles Pendrill, London Life in the Fourteenth Century (New
York, n. d.), p. 105.
43* Henry B. Wheatley, The Story of London (London, 1904), p. 313.
44* Ibid.
45* Henry P. Maskell and Edward W. Gregory, Old Country Inns of
England (Boston, 1911), p. 62.
46* Hackwood, p. 81.
47* Francis X. Weiser, Handbook of Christian Feasts and Customs
(New York, 1952), pp. 305-306; E. O. James, Seasonal Feasts and
Festivals (New York, 1961), p. 238; Maurice Vloberg, Les Fêtes de
France (Grenoble/Paris, 1942), p. 175f.
48* Réau, loc. cit. ; III, pt. 3 (Paris, 1959), 1453-1482.
49* Emile Mâle, The Gothic Image, trans. Dora Nussey. (New York,
1958), p. 270.
50* Corblet, IV, 128f.
51* Réau, n. 47, supra.
52* Anna Jameson, Sacred and Legendary Art (Boston, 1896), II,
781.
53* Ibid.
54* White, p. 29; Jameson, II, pp. 779, 762.
55* Arthur de Bles, How to Distinguish the Saints in Art (New York,
1925), pp. 11, 109, 144, 151; R. L. P. Milburn, Saints and Their
Emblems in English Churches (Oxford, 1961), p. 2; Francis Bond,
Dedications of English Churches: Ecclesiastical Symbolism, Saints
and Their Emblems (London, 1914), pp. 292, 297, 298, 301, 308;
Helen Roeder, Saints and Their Attributes (Chicago, 1956), p. 18;
F. R. Webber, Church Symbolism (Cleveland, 1938), pp. 265, 287;
Otto Wimmer, Handbuch der Namen und Heiligen (Innsbruck/Wien/
München, 1953), pp. 241-242, 267; Corblet, IV, 128-130; Künstle,
pp. 31-32; Holweck, pp. 19-20; Réau, III, pt. 3, 1424.
56* G. H. Cook, Portrait of Canterbury Cathedral (New York, 1949),

pp. 47, 327–328; see also E. W. Tristram, English Wall-Painting of the Fourteenth Century, London, 1955.

57* Réau, III, pt. 1, 24, points out an eroneous identification of St. Loy for St. Adrian by Westlake, History of Design in Painted Glass, IV, 64.

58* Arthur Hussey, Testamenta Cantiana: A Series of Extracts from Fifteenth and Sixteenth Century Wills Relating to Church Building and Topography (Kent Archaeological Society), Extra Vol. (London, 1907), x, 7.

59* Archaeologica Cantiana, Kent Archaeological Society, X (London, 1876), xlix.

60* Jacques de Voragine, La Légende Dorée (Paris, 1843), I, 374; transl. in Butler's Lives, III, 507.

61* Butler's Lives, III, 508; Analecta Bollandiana, 79 (1961), 15, note additionnelle.

62* Légende Dorée, I, 376.

63* See n. 54, supra.

2

THE PARDONER'S ST. RONYAN*

The St. Ronyan oaths in the Physician-Pardoner link (Canterbury Tales, C 310, 320) 1* have generated research 'an heep.' Scholarly energies have been concentrated on (1) showing that an alternate name for Ronyan was Ninian, 2* and (2) treating the name as the common noun runian, meaning 'kidney,' 'farm hand,' 'testicle' or 'scab,' 3* having first, long ago, dismissed from consideration the simplest identification of Ronyan: St. Ronan. The equation 'Ronyan sometimes equals Ninian' is convincing, but the appropriateness of Ninian for Chaucer's Pardoner is not. The reason offered as proof of St. Ninian's suitability is that, according to a nineteenth century source, it was Ninian's practice to fast from Holy Thursday till after the Easter Mass, a habit inconsonant with the tavern setting where the Pardoner swore by Ronyan, since "Easter was just past or at hand." 4* Fasting is a standard occupation of saints and, as will be shown below, is hardly unique with Ninian. Further, the very piece of scholarship that equates Ronyan and Ninian names the fasts of several other saints; any fasting saint would have suited the situation. Therefore the claim that "no more incongruous saint than Ninian could be imagined" 5* is simply unfounded.

Not only does the first line of scholarship listed above fail to demonstrate the peculiar suitability of Ninian for the Pardoner, but the disposal of the second as a condition for its acceptance is unnecessary. Chaucer is not so simple a poet that he cannot have more than one level of meaning in operation. The use of runian as a common noun is not implausible. The definition of the word as 'scab' seems particularly homogenous, in fact, with the Physician-oriented context of C 310, following the anatomical lines 304-307; further, it is a three-syllable word, as is here required. Another of the definitions, 'testicle,' is not only anatomical but forms a balance with the "coillons" reference near the end of the tale (C 952).

Adherents of the approaches discussed above demand an all-or--nothing acceptance and in so doing are eager to dispose of the possible identification of St. Ronan with the saint in one or both of the oaths. Sledd hastily sweeps Ronan under the rug with one brief paragraph. His dismissal is completely negative scholarship: we do not understand, ergo it cannot be. He quotes Skeat as "admitting that 'of St. Ronan scarcely anything is known,' " hurrying on to conclude with Manly's comment that " 'nothing we know of St. Ronan explains the choice of the oath.' " 6* However, the facts still remain that 1. 320 does require a two-syllable word to rhyme with "anon" and St. Ronan must be left open for consideration until or unless it can be demon-

*Margaretta Henry Soyez has generously shared her research with me throughout this chapter and the following one.

strated that he is not suitable.

Sledd has contended further that "if there is any significance in the Pardoner's alteration of the name [C 310's three-syllable name as opposed to the two-syllable saint's name in 320], I do not see it. Chaucer constantly uses variant forms of proper names for the sake of metre and rhyme. " 7* First of all, the variation of names in Chaucer usually applies to characters in the tales, not saints in oaths who are mentioned only once or twice. While it is true that the language, not only of Chaucer but of all of English, has easily adapted to the presence or absence of a syllable - one can frequently find two-syllable <u>heaven</u> and one-syllable <u>heav'n</u> sharing the same hymn verse - it is also a fact that the process of paronomasia has produced some of the cleverest lines in English. For example, see <u>Romeo</u> I. i. 1-5: <u>colliers</u>, <u>choler</u>, <u>collar</u>. Helge Kökeritz has shown that in Chaucer's literary heritage of "classical and post-classical rhetoric, several forms of word-play, or paranomasia, were legitimate ornaments of style, " 8* and has supplied abundant examples of such usage. The possibility for punning and word-play in the Physician-Pardoner link must not be ruled out. Unless he had especially wanted to use Ronyan/Ronyon, Chaucer could easily have found a second saint's name for C 320 or have omitted the reference altogether, as is demonstrated by the variant readings of the line. 9* But Chaucerian satire simply does not operate on throwaway lines, as the referential oaths for which we now have satisfactory explanations attest. Therefore it would seem discreet to believe what the text says before we decide it really says something else: 1. 320 clearly ends "by St. Rŏn-yón. "

A fresh appraisal seems in order and I will begin with two premises: first, that Chaucer took advantage of the opportunities for satire which he himself had created, and second, that those names which vary least from preferred manuscript tradition should be given first consideration. It is impossible to guess why the Ronan of Ronan's Well fame was the only saint of this name considered, especially for C 320, over the years. Perhaps the researchers were trying to limit themselves to saints within Great Britain or to saints whose lives were factual. The first reason seems strange in the face of Chaucer's use of non-British saints such as St. Loy, St. Joce and St. Nicholas. The second, though a point of legitimate concern to hagiographers, matters 'not a groat' when dealing with popular knowledge of a saint. Legends, accreted through art, drama, general folklore, confusion with other saints, and puns are all that need concern us here. We are interested in what came to the medieval mind when a saint's name was mentioned. The Scottish Runyon/ Rinnian/Ninian saints seem remote from Chaucer's continentally oriented ecclesiastical world. We know little of the <u>vita</u> of the Breton St. Ronon, but his <u>legend,</u> which had been gathering lore for centuries even in Chaucer's lifetime, seems very appropriate for consideration and Chaucer's knowledge of it is quite probable. Though confusion among saints named Ronan/Ronyan/Ruman is easily the the greatest in hagiography, 10* we will here consider the lore attached to the name on a geographical basis, i. e. , in Brittany. 11*

St. Ronan, a Celt, came to pre-Christian Brittany early, perhaps
in the fifth century, sailing to the treacherous coastal area on a rock
called the Stone Mare. 12* The non-Christian inhabitants of the area
of Leon, who made their living as pirates and scavengers of the ships
that foundered on the rocks, came to hate Ronan, who warned the men
at sea of their peril by means of a bell. And to Ronan also was attributed control over the elements. The saint decided to seek more
hospitable territory and, traveling through thick forests with the
Stone Mare, was able to command the dense growth to part and make
a path for them by ringing his bell. He came to the area of the Bay
of Douarnenez and settled at what became Locronan, 'the place of
Ronan.' 13* In the new area, too, he acquired an unsavory reputation: he was known as a werewolf, controller of the elements, and a
sorcerer. One Keben, variously designated as 'witch' or 'virago,'
was his special adversary, because he took away her husband to be
a hermit. When she attempted to retrieve her husband from St. Ronan,
dubbed "the Ravisher of Men, " he warned her to "beware the circle
of holly, which no woman may cross. " 14* Except for Keben's husband, Ronan had no human contacts and was protected against in-
trusion by the Stone Mare and a thick spider web. Walking his long,
penitential route alone daily, regardless of weather, he fasted until
the whole circuit was completed. When Ronan died, men despaired
of burying him, for fear of his visiting a curse on them for choosing
the wrong place. They put his body on a cart pulled by oxen, and the
Stone Mare (and in some versions oxen) led them to the spot of
Ronan's choice, whereupon the bier, body and trees overhead, which
formed the shape of arches, petrified and a church formed over the
burial place. On the way to the interment, the witch Keben, who had
struck the saint's face, was instantly obliterated through the power
of the dead saint and a grim, monolithic stone sprang up to mark her
grave.(The women of the area are still reputed to be Keben-like and
must atone for Keben's offense each year on the saint's feast day.)
    Stone is a prominent symbol of Ronan's legend. The Stone Mare
is the saint's inseparable companion. He sailed to Brittany on the
Mare, and she was his constant companion, the only creature who
could determine his burial spot after his death without fearing his
wrath. She guarded him during his sleep and gave up her animation
at his death, which suggests something close to a theriomorphic
existence. The Stone Mare became, in strange contrast with the
cold hermit-saint, a fertility shrine similar to those discussed by
Adriaan DeGroot in relation to St. Nicholas. 15* In much the same
fashion as with the Nicholas shrines, actual physical contact was
made between barren women and the stone.
    In addition to being the material of the Mare, stone reminds us of
the saint's ability to petrify people and objects. Keben was rendered
unable to move - "as if turned to stone" - when she tried to cross
the circle of holly in which her husband was contained. And the bier,
trees and saint himself were turned to stone ultimately. The saint
had the power to render powerless and unregenerate, as if dead, that
which he willed. Not only had he the ability to petrify, but his legend
contains references to his power over the elements and, thereby,

power over the growing of food and, hence, life itself. Although saints ordinarily become more saintly with the passage of time, even current lore of St. Ronan still refers to his unpleasantness and distance from other humans.

Holly is also important in the legend of Ronan, being the tree of which his excluding circle was composed. Although holly is sometimes simply a symbol of masculinity, as in the traditional holly and ivy carols, in connection with Ronan it is sexually excluding. Keben is told that no woman might cross the holly to approach the saint. The antagonism of Ronan toward all humans, particularly women, is, in fact, found throughout his legend. Even today women must try to placate the saint, dead for centuries. In his role as Yule-king, Saturn had a Saturnalia club of holly, it will be remembered, and "On Yule morning, the last of his merry reign, the first foot over the threshold had to be that of Saturn's representative, a dark man, called the Holly Boy, and elaborate precautions were taken to keep women out of the way. " 16*

It would seem, then, that the holly of St. Ronan's legend should be regarded not as a symbol of regeneration, but, rather, an agent for deterring regeneration. As Moore has pointed out in his discussion of the English carols, the holly is not either masculine or feminine, but is, rather, dioecious. 17* In its bisexuality it represents the self-contained hermit who wants no contact with women particularly, or humans generally, except with the person he has brought within the holly circle, another man.

The affinities between St. Ronan and his legend and the Pardoner and his tale are especially striking at this point. Initially, the place of women in both stories is similar: the witch Keben is the only woman in the saint's legend, and women appear in the Pardoner's Tale only as temptations (C 477, 478, 479). Further, the cold, isolated characters of the Pardoner and St. Ronan are similar. The description of the Pardoner reveals immediately that something is sexually amiss with the man, but what that something may be is not so clear. Beryl Rowland has demonstrated that the Pardoner is hermaphroditic, like the holly, dioecious. Physically he is a testicular pseudo-hermaphrodite of the feminine type, " 18* and we know he is emotionally involved in a homosexual liaison with the Summoner. 19* One of the indications of the Pardoner's abnormality is the line "I trowe he were a geldyng or a mare" (A 691), and it is interesting that Ronan's stone was specifically designated mare, rather than just horse. The Pardoner's oath by a saint whose symbol and legend suggest the same physical and emotional deviations he suffers, is striking.

St. Ronan's holly symbolism offers a link between the saint and the Pardoner not only for its bisexuality, but through its connection with Saturn, as we have seen. The figure of Saturn is especially apt in connection with the Pardoner's Tale because of its evolution into Father Time-Death-Old Age. 20* Panofsky has dealt with the evolution of the figure from Cronos-Saturn onward, and a look at his discussion of the symbolism surrounding the figure seems appropriate.

First of all, Saturn's devouring a baby 21* reminds us of the unregenerative aspect of both the Pardoner and St. Ronan, particularly in the later representations in which the baby becomes a stone, 22* the symbol of the Ronan legend first discussed. The unregenerative aspect of Saturn is omnipresent in the figure because of the sickle or scythe, the instrument of his emasculation. 23* Among the Saturnine types are the hermit 24* and the miser. 25* Death, at the opposite pole from life and regeneration, is also frequently represented in depictions of the Saturnine. Further, we learn, the Saturnine may be wise but are always unhappy, 26* the condition of the Pardoner. Penseroso, therefore, is Saturnine, and Panofsky, in discussing a representation of the figure, comments on its "Saturnian silence, " 27* and notes that his elbow "rests on a closed cash-box, a typical symbol of Saturnian parsimony, " 28* and in another instance notes that "Saturn is shown holding the keys to a closed strong-box. " 29* In still another instance, "the melancholic sets out to bury a strong-box filled with money and the attributes of a purse and/or a table covered with coins is ubiquitous in representations both of Saturn and the melancholic. " 30* The implications of the sermon of the Pardoner, in which Radix malorum est Cupiditas is the theme, and the tale, wherein melancholy, death, age and avarice are connected, hardly needs stressing. 31*

It should be noted that the St. Ronan legend has other ties with the Pardoner's Tale as well. The holly, a symbol found in the legend, is traditionally equated with the evergreen oak, such as the scarlet-oak, kerm-oak, and holly-oak. Both are designated ilex-. 32* The oak is the tree mentioned in C 765 of the Pardoner's Tale. 33* In connection with Chaucer's "ook, " the ritual of burying death has been discussed, 34* but the tree has wider meaning as well. First of all, the oak is a symbol of age and endurance and in this sense has affinities with the old man in the tale. The oak, further, implies the world-tree, one of the regions beneath which is that of the dead. 35* The tree is equated with a road up to heaven (the limbs) and a road down to hell (the roots), "a tedious and fearsome road down to the abode of the dead. " 36* Compare the instructions of the old man to the three rioters: "To fynde Deeth, turne up this croked wey, / For in that grove I lafte hym, by my fey, / Under a tree" (761-763), described two lines later as "that ook. "

The presence of trees in both the St. Ronan legend and the Pardoner's Tale is significant not only for the holly and oak specifically, but in a broader sense. The presence of trees in these stories furthers the symbolism of hermaphroditism. Jung, in discussing the relationship of trees and bisexuality, notes that the symbolism "is also suggested by the fact that in Latin the names of trees have masculine endings and the feminine gender. " 37*

Another symbol of the St. Ronan legend is the spider web, which protected the entrance to the hermit's cell. The spider, especially within its web, represents self-containment, as well as death and avarice. 38* "Those who have become the slaves of the passions live wholly in them, moving about in a world of illusions, the creation of their own desires, as the spider runs to and fro on the filaments of the web, which it has spun out of its own bowels. " 39* Even the

spider's begetting came in for comment. T. H. White's translation of
a twelfth century Latin bestiary comments that "the worm is an
animal which is mostly germinated, without sexual intercourse." 40*
Renaissance commentary on the spider is always derogatory. For
example, in a sixteenth century source we read, " 'verely as spiders
convert to poison whatsoever they touche, so women infect with folly
whom so ever they deale withall,' " 41* and the spider's evil nature
is constantly reiterated in the familiar idea that a bee and a spider,
sucking from the same flower, will extract honey and poison respectively. 42*

There are other symbols of the Ronan legend which are related to
the tale, the wolf, for example. This animal, sometimes found with
the saint in graphic representations and linked with him in the expression "gentle as St. Ronon's wolf, " is explained as a symbol of
the saint's having cleared a wilderness. 43* But the wolf is much more
importantly a symbol of avarice. 44* The symbolism continues today,
of course, in such expressions as "keeping the wolf from the door."
Jung mentions the wolf as a world destroyer, 45* and Panofsky dis-
cusses the personification of Greed as a wolf. 46* The symbol appears
in Chaucer's translation of the De Consolatione Philosophiae of
Boethius, IV, m. 3, pr. 3. Further, mention should be made of the
bell of St. Ronan, with which he is invariably represented. The bell
forms an aural link with the Pardoner's Tale, where it is rung to
announce the passing of the funeral: "they herde a belle clynke/ Bi-
forn a cors, was caried to his grave" (C 664-665).

The legend of St. Ronan is viable even today. The festival of this
saint, a patron of Brittany, is still celebrated each year at Locronan,
as it has been since the twelfth century. The feast occurs on the
second Sunday of July, and every sixth year it lasts for eight days.
The longer feast, the Grand Tromenie, is an important Breton event
known as the Pardon of the Mountain. It includes making a long,
mountainous circuit, the pilgrims struggling to climb just once in
six years the difficult path which St. Ronan purportedly walked every
day, fasting as he went. The pilgrims who complete the tour gain an
indulgence as their reward. 47*

It is interesting to wonder if Chaucer, while he was in France in
the spring and summer of 1377, 48* might have known of the pardon,
since one of the major celebrations took place in that year. It is also
worth noting that another of the Grand Tromenies was celebrated in
1395, the possible year during which the Pardoner's Tale was being
written. One of the factors which adds particular interest to this
speculation is the region of the festival, of which Chaucer seems to
have had some knowledge. Locronan is situated in Finistere, only a
few miles from Penmarch (Pedmark), the scene of the Franklin's
Tale. 49*

NOTES

1* All quotations are from The Works of Geoffrey Chaucer, ed.
F. N. Robinson, 2nd ed. (Cambridge, 1957).

2* James Sledd, "Canterbury Tales, C 310, 320: 'By Seint Ronyan,' " Mediaeval Studies, XIII (1951), 226-233. See notes for references to previous scholarship on these oaths.

3* Robinson, p. 728, n. to C 310; Sledd, 228-230.

4* Sledd, 233.

5* Sledd, 233.

6* Sledd, 228.

7* Sledd, 233, n. 40.

8* "Rhetorical Word-Play in Chaucer," PMLA, LXIX (1954), 938.

9* John M. Manly and Edith Rickert, The Text of the Canterbury Tales, (Chicago, 1940), VII, 37f.

10* Alban Butler's Lives of the Saints, eds. H. Thurston and D. Attwater (New York, 1956), III, 447-448, assesses the confusion. See also: F. G. Holweck, A Biographical Dictionary of the Saints (St. Louis, 1924), pp. 867-868; Paul Grosjean, "Vie de S. Rumon, Vie, Invention et Miracles de S. Nectan," Analecta Bollandiana, LXXI (1953), 359-414; Gilbert H. Doble, St. Rumon and St. Ronan, Cornish Saints Series, No. 42 (Shipston-on-Stour, 1939), and for a strikingly opposed point of view, John Whitaker, The Ancient Cathedral of Cornwall, II (London, 1804), p. 188f; Sabine Baring-Gould, Lives of the British Saints (London, 1913), IV, 120-125; Louis Réau, Iconographie de l'art Chrétien, III, Pt. 3 (1959), 1169. Fr. Grosjean's notes are particularly helpful.

11* Hippolyte Delehaye, The Legends of the Saints, tr. Donald Attwater (New York, 1962), p. 7 and Chap. II, "The Production of Legend."

12* Anatole le Braz, The Land of Pardons, tr. Frances M. Gostling (New York, 1906), pp. 198-248; Louis Gougaud, Les Saints irlandais hors d'Irland (Louvain, 1936), pp. 159-166, and translation of earlier edition contained in Gaelic Pioneers of Christianity, tr. Victor Collins (Dublin, 1923); Amy Oakley, Enchanted Brittany (New York, 1930), pp. 221-237; Katharine S. Macquoid, Through Brittany (London, c. 1880), p. 313ff.; Michelin et Cie, Brittany, English ed. for 1966, p. 116f.; Lucien Lheureux, Bretagne (Paris, 1920), p. 578.

13* W. B. S. Smith, "De la Toponymie Bretonne," Language, XVI (1940), 115.

14* le Braz, Pardons, p. 212.

15* Adriaan D. DeGroot, Saint Nicholas: A Psychoanalytic Study of His History and Myth (The Hague/Paris, 1965), p. 109. Paul-Yves Sébillot, Le Folklore de la Bretagne, II (Paris, 1968), p. 93f.

16* Robert Graves, The White Goddess (New York, 1948), p. 153.

17* Arthur K. Moore, "Mixed Tradition in the Carols of Holly and Ivy," Modern Language Notes, LXII (1947), 554-556.

18* "Animal Imagery and the Pardoner's Abnormality," Neophilologus, XLVIII (1964), 56-60.

19* Alfred David, "Criticism and the Old Man in Chaucer's Pardoner's Tale," College English, XXVII (1965), 43 and n. 14; see also Ernst R. Curtius, European Literature and the Latin Middle Ages, tr. Willard R. Trask (New York, 1953), p. 113: "Only a fluid boundary separates [hermaphroditism] from male homosexuality, which was also widespread in the Middle Ages."

24

20* I am not equating Chaucer's Old Man with Saturn, but in a very general sense it is safe to observe that he is old and nearer death than the other characters in the tale, and has affinities with Saturn.
21* Erwin Panofsky, Studies in Iconology (New York, 1962), pp. 74, 78.
22* Panofsky, p. 79, n. 36.
23* Panofsky, pp. 74, 78.
24* Panofsky, p. 77.
25* Panofsky, pp. 82, 79, 69f.
26* Panofsky, p. 76f.
27* Panofsky, p. 211 and n. 118.
28* Panofsky, p. 211.
29* Panofsky, p. 211 and n. 119.
30* Panofsky, p. 211 and n. 119. These attributes are, of course, time-honored symbols of avarice. See, for example, Émile Mâle, The Gothic Image, tr. Dora Nussey (New York, 1958), p. 100f.
31* There is an implicit funereal feeling throughout the entire body of Ronan lore. See, for example, Anatole le Braz, La Légende de Mort (Paris, 1922), II, Chap. XV, "Les pelerinages des âmes," 89-90 and n. 2; and Eleanor Clark, "Brittany: Dragon Country," Vogue (October, 1964).
32* Graves, pp. 149-150.
33* le Braz, Pardons, pp. 205-206, relates a legend of St. Ronan and an oak tree; Sébillot, "Le culte des arbres," II, p. 107f.
34* Frederick H. Candelaria, "Chaucer's fowle Ok" and The Pardoner's Tale," LXXI (1956), 321-322; Robert A. Barakat, "Odin: Old Man of The Pardoner's Tale," Southern Folklore Quarterly, XXVIII (1964), 211f.
35* H. R. Ellis Davidson, Gods and Myths of Northern Europe (Harmondsworth/Baltimore, 1964), pp. 191-193.
36* Davidson, p. 193.
37* C. G. Jung, Symbols of Transformation, Bollingen Series XX (New York, 1956), p. 221.
38* J. E. Cirlot, A Dictionary of Symbols, tr. Jack Sage (London/New York, 1962), p. 49; George Ferguson, Signs and Symbols in Christian Art (New York, 1966), p. 24; E. W. Tristram, English Wall Painting of the Fourteenth Century (London, 1955), p. 106; Morton W. Bloomfield, The Seven Deadly Sins (East Lansing, 1952), p. 189.
39* E. P. Evans, Animal Symbolism in Ecclesiastical Architecture (New York, 1896), p. 32.
40* T. H. White, The Bestiary (New York, 1954), p. 191.
41* William M. Carroll, Animal Conventions in English Renaissance Non-Religious Prose, 1550-1600 (New York, 1954), p. 53.
42* Carroll, pp. 65, 77, 133.
43* Anna Jameson, Legends of the Monastic Orders (New York, 1901) p. 18.
44* Adolf Katzenellenbogen, Allegories of the Virtues and Vices in Mediaeval Art (New York, 1964), p. 61.
45* Jung, Symbols, p. 438.
46* Panofsky, p. 84, n. 60.

47* Howell Walker, "France Meets the Sea in Brittany," National Geographic, CXXVII (1965), 482f.; and see n.12 (above).

48* M. M. Crow and C. C. Olson, Chaucer Life Records (Austin, 1966), pp. 44-45; 558-561, etc.

49* J. S. P. Tatlock, The Scene of the Franklin's Tale Visited (London, 1914), Chaucer Society, 2nd Series, no. 51.

3

THE ST. GILES OATH IN THE CANON'S YEOMAN'S TALE*

The oath sworn by St. Giles in the Canon's Yeoman's Tale (G1185), 1*
both decorates and illuminates: it functions as a highly appropriate
ornament for the tale and as a microcosmic reflection of the major
themes in the tale. On the first, most obvious level, that of ornamen-
tation, the oath adds support to the characterization of alchemists as
social aliens. St. Giles, one of the Fourteen Helpers in Western
Christendom, had a widely disseminated legend which earned him the
specific patronage of cripples, beggars, blacksmiths, lepers, and
epileptics 2* and, in general, "of those struck by some sudden misery,
and driven into solitude." 3* The appropriateness of Giles for a practitioner of the suspect science of alchemy is obvious. There had long
been periodic surges of protest against alchemy, but its illegality in
England after 1403 4* bespeaks the especially strong distrust of alchemists in the last part of Chaucer's life when the Canon's Yeoman's Tale
was written.

St. Giles was one of the best known saints in the Middle Ages, particularly because of the pilgrimage to the abbey which bore his name
and which was under the patronage of the Counts of Toulouse, the
"Comtes de Saint-Gilles." 5* This pilgrimage was popular in part
because of its location on the routes to both Santiago de Compostella
and Rome, 6* and there are records of visits by several famous people.
For example, the ailing St. Louis celebrated Pentecost at St. Giles
during a ten day stop at the abbey in 1270. 7* This saint's popularity in
England is easily discernible by the number of dedications to him there
8* and also by the various ancient St. Giles fairs. 9*

In keeping with the tradition of hidden meaning and symbolism in
alchemical writings, the St. Giles oath is also appropriate to the tale
beyond its mere surface. The context in which the oath occurs gives
a clue to further meaning. When the Canon has placed the two elements,
the prima materia, in the crucible and the fire has been applied, 10*
he says to the priest, "Now lat me medle therwith but a while, / For
of yow have I pitee, by Seint Gile!" The word medle denotes, first,
'stir, mix (in),' according to the OED. But to meddle had the additional
meaning 'to have sexual intercourse (with),' a sense which is completely consonant with alchemical sexual terminology, by which the
whole process is seen as an allegory of regeneration. At the point in
the tale at which the oath occurs, the male sulphur and the female
mercury have been placed in the crucible for the purpose of repro-
ducing the higher offspring metal, the alchemist himself being the
agent who brings about the fertilization. 11* Since the offspring was
actually produced by the crafty Canon to dupe the priest, this was

* Most of the material in this chapter has appeared in Chaucer Review, VII, 1973.

"meddling" without "multiplication" and was, therefore, a sin.

The concept of spiritual multiplication has been discussed adequately in connection with both the Pardoner and the Canon's Yeoman's Tale.12* While the Canon's Yeoman gives a catalogue of reasons for his failure to produce silver and gold in the alchemical process (G 922-954), his list includes only mechanical faults, not spiritual omissions. The spiritual preparation of the practitioner's soul was as important as the practical preparation of the materials for the work, and cleanness, or chastity, was a part of the preparation. In the Aurora Consurgens, for example, a quotation from Alphidius advises "Know, that thou canst not have this science, unless thou shalt purify thy mind before God, that is, wipe away all corruption from thy heart." 13* This advice accompanies a list of fourteen virtues requisite for the alchemist, one of which is chastity. 14* In Forgerons et Alchimistes Mircea Eliade, discussing taboos among mine workers, shows that the belief in a relationship between miners' spiritual cleanness - especially as demonstrated through sexual abstinence - and the success of their work is still a viable concept. 15*

Since the relative purity of the alchemical practitioner was directly operable on the purification of the metal - variously described as "impure," "sick," "sinful" or "dirty" - which needed to be cleansed, purified, made unsinful or healthy to become gold, the clean spiritual state specified for the alchemist is frequently compared to physical health. Conversely, physical disease or deformity was symbolic of spiritual disease. Jung quotes Geber: "But if the body of the 'artist' is weak and sick, like bodies of people with fever or leprosy, whose limbs fall off, or like the bodies of people laboring at the end of their life, or of old men of decrepit age, he will not achieve the completion of the Art." 16* The metaphor of the cleansing of the leper is encountered frequently in connection with spiritual cleanness of the alchemist. 17* "The leper was considered an image for the heretic. In alchemy and in the Cabala the story of Naaman [2 Kings 5: iff.] was applied to the leprositas of the metals." 18* Sometimes the sickness of the material ("lead is really gold into which sickness has penetrated") is labelled as epilepsy or hydrophobia. 19*

How does St. Giles relate to all of this? First, this saint was the patron of lepers, as mentioned earlier. And leprosy was frequently medically linked with venereal disease.20* In fact, syphilis, confused with leprosy, was sometimes known as "St. Giles' Disease." 21* In the medieval scheme of things, sins were equated with diseases, and although "disease and sin have always been closely linked... disease-sin linkages became increasingly common throughout the Middle Ages."22* In this pattern, lechery is represented by leprosy, so that a patron saint of lepers is also patron of lechers. 23* Indeed, in addition to the symbolism of lechery for leprosy and the medical confusion of venereal disease and leprosy, leprosy was sometimes believed to be the actual result of lechery. 24* Further, St. Giles' patronage of epileptics 25* is linked to these beliefs, epilepsy sometimes being associated with lechery, 26* although epilepsy was thought to be the result of sexual repression. 27* St. Giles' connection with the disease of leprosy, in particular, is seen in the several hospitals for lepers dedicated to him, St. Giles, Cripplegate, being especially close to Chaucer. 28*

Secondly, through the herb fennel, an attribute of St. Giles, there is another connection between the saint and the tale. According to most of the early herbals, in addition to other medical uses, fennel was used both as an aphrodisiac and to promote fertility, 29* as well as against sterility of women. 30* Falstaff's reference to "conger and fennel" (2 H. IV II. iv. 267), along with mention of the herb by Jonson and Green, illustrates its continued reputation as an aphrodisiac. 31* The stalk of fennel was used as a container for fire and as fuel itself. Fire, one of the four basic elements and an integral part of the alchemical process, is historically associated with fennel, since Prometheus was supposed to have carried fire to the people in a fennel stalk. 32* Frazer refers to it frequently in relation to the Midsummer's Eve, or St. John's fire, to the smoke of which was exposed everything imaginable - crops, human beings, animals - to promote good health and fertility. 33* And it was also hung over doors along with St. John's Wort on Midsummer's Eve, presumably for the same reasons. 34*

Third, the St. Giles legend of the remitted sin was popular in the fourteenth century. (It is represented three times at Chartres alone.) According to that story, clearly anachronistic but in currency for some time before Chaucer, Charlemagne besought St. Giles' aid in remission of a sin so terrible that he could not even confess it. After much intercession on the part of the saint, a paper was delivered from heaven, granting pardon to Charlemagne and, thereby, bestowing on Giles the reputation of power to pardon unconfessed but earnestly repented sins. The sin of Charlemagne was reputed to have been an incestuous relationship with his sister Gisèle, certainly "meddling" without intention to multiply. 35* A branch of the sin of lechery, 36* incest seems to have held a particular fascination for the later Middle Ages, as may be seen in, for example, Gower's Confessio Amantis. And in alchemical treatises, "the brother-sister pair stands allegorically for the whole conception of opposites, " 37* the figure of royal incest being especially prominent.

A few other aspects of St. Giles' appropriateness to the Canon's Yeoman's Tale should be mentioned. In early herbals, St. Giles' attribute fennel is invariably listed as an ingredient in medications for eye diseases, for instance. 38* The Yeoman is privy only to the secrets of exoteric, rather than esoteric alchemy, to begin with, and there are numerous specific allusions to blindness and sight in the tale, as is shown in Bruce Rosenberg's discussion. 39*

Rosenberg's theory of opposites for the tales of the Second Nun and the Canon's Yeoman is helpful in examining the St. Giles oath in several instances. It adds a dimension to the theme of "meddling," discussed already. The spiritual fruitfulness of the clean, or chaste, marriage of Cecilia and Valerian represents multiplication without meddling, whereas the fruitlessness of the unclean, or lecherous, alchemical union over which the Canon presides constitutes meddling without multiplication. Further, Rosenberg's discussion of the word "work" in the two tales, prompts us to look at the usage in light of the Giles oath. The sexual implications of St. Giles' legend and patronage extend the meaning of the word in the Canon's Yeoman's Tale even more. John

Read refers to the alchemists as "labourers in the fire, " 40* an apt expression which can be interpreted as 'those who propagate alchemically.' In this sense, "work" has the sexual connotation of work or labor as in the Merchant's Tale, in, for example, ' "Ther nys no werkman, whatsoevere he be, / That may bothe werke wel and hastily" ' (E 1831-1832), ' "Thus laboureth he til that the day gan dawe" ' (E 1942), or ' "But heere I lete hem werken in hir wyse" ' (E 1965).

In the Canon's Yeoman's Tale Chaucer has skillfully intertwined the sins of avarice and lechery, lust for material gain and spiritual lust. (Chaucer uses the opposite concept, spiritual chastity, in the Physician's Tale, C 43: "As wel in goost as body chast. ") The two sins of avarice and lechery are traditionally linked, as Bloomfield shows frequently, 41* culminating in their actual teaming as a pair, riding together in The Faerie Queene (I. iv. 24-29). And Chaucer has mentioned the two sins together in the Parson's Tale, in which avarice is defined as "a likerousnesse in herte" (I 741). In the Second Nun's Tale St. Cecilia represents not only charity, opposing avarice in the Canon's Yeoman's Tale, but also chastity, the traditionally mitigating virtue for lechery, underscored by the St. Giles oath.

NOTES

1* Citations are from The Works of Geoffrey Chaucer, ed. F. N. Robinson, 2nd ed. (Boston, 1957).
2* F. Brittain, Saint Giles (Cambridge, Eng. , 1928); Legenda Aurea, ed. Theodor Graesse (Dresden, 1846), pp. 582-584, and the translation by Helmut Rippenger and Granger Ryan (New York, 1941), II, 516-519; Alban Butler's Lives of the Saints, eds. H. Thurston and D. Attwater (New York, 1956), III, 457-458; Sabine Baring-Gould, Lives of the Saints, rev. ed. (London, 1914), X, 8-10; F. G. Holweck, A Biographical Dictionary of the Saints (London/St. Louis, 1924), p. 22; J. Corblet, Hagiographie du diocese d'Amiens, IV (Paris/Amiens, 1874), 303-305; Louis Réau, Iconographie de l'art chrétien, III, Pt. 2 (Paris, 1958), 593-597. The character of these references is decidedly legendary, in the sense set out by Hippolyte Delehaye (The Legends of the Saints, tr. Donald Attwater (New York, 1962), pp. 7-8), rather than factual.

3* Anna Jameson, Sacred and Legendary Art (Boston, 1896), II, 393.
4* The Canon's Yeoman's Prologue and Tale, ed. Maurice Hussey (Cambridge, 1965), p. 10.
5* Anna Jameson, Legends of the Monastic Orders (New York, 1890), p. 29.
6* Réau, 594; Rippenger and Ryan, 518-519; A. T. Baker, "Saints Lives Written in Anglo-French, " Essays by Divers Hands, Transactions of the Royal Society of Literature, n. s. , IV (1924), 128-129; Holweck, p. 22.
7* Margaret W. Labarge, Saint Louis (Boston, 1968), pp. 236-238.
8* R. L. P. Milburn, Saints and Their Emblems in English Churches, (Oxford, 1961), p. 116; Francis Bond, Dedications of English Churches, (London, 1914), pp. 176-177.

30

9* W. C. Hazlitt, Faiths and Folklore of the British Isles (New York, 1965), I, 274; Dorothy G. Spicer, Yearbook of English Festivals (New York, 1954), p. 119; A. R. Wright, British Calendar Customs, Publications of the Folk-Lore Society (London/Glasgow, 1940), III, 58ff.
10* Paull F. Baum, "The Canon's Yeoman's Tale," MLN, XL (1925), 152-154, explains the order of the alchemical process in the tale.
11* Serge Hutin, A History of Alchemy, tr. Tamara Alferoff (New York, 1962), p. 34.
12* Joseph E. Grennen, "The Canon's Yeoman and the Cosmic Furnace Language and Meaning in the "Canon's Yeoman's Tale," Criticism, IV (1962), 225-240, and Robert P. Miller, "Chaucer's Pardoner, the Scriptural Eunuch, and the Pardoner's Tale," Speculum, XXX (1955), 180-199.
13* Aurora Consurgens, ed. Marie-Louise von Franz, tr. R. F. C. Hull and A. S. B. Glover (London, 1966), pp. 106-107, and n. 32.
14* Aurora, pp. 104ff.; see also Carl G. Jung, Psychology and Alchemy, tr. R. F. C. Hull (New York, 1953), pp. 258-259.
15* (Paris, 1956), Chapter 5, especially pp. 60, 61-62.
16* Jung, pp. 243-244.
17* Aurora, pp. 310ff.
18* Aurora, p. 312.
19* Aurora, p. 313.
20* Thomas J. Garbáty, "The Summoner's Occupational Disease," Medical History, VII (1963), 348-358.
21* Benjamin L. Gordon, Medieval and Renaissance Medicine (London, 1960), p. 524; John Lowe, "Comments on the History of Leprosy," Indian Medical Gazette, XXXIII (1942), 684.
22* Morton Bloomfield, The Seven Deadly Sins (East Lansing, 1952), p. 355, n. 6.
23* Bloomfield, pp. 195-196, cites Gower's Mirour de l'omme.
24* Bloomfield, pp. 176-177.
25* Réau, 595.
26* Bloomfield, p. 373.
27* Maurice Bassan, "Chaucer's Cursed Monk, Constantinus Africanus," Mediaeval Studies, XXIV (1962), 134.
28* Jameson, Sac. and Leg. Art, 393n.; D. W. Robertson, Jr., Chaucer's London (London, 1968), p. 68.
29* Encyclopaedia Londinensis, comp. John Wilkes (London, 1810), VIII, 336; Agnus Castus, A M. E. Herbal, ed. Gösta Brodin, Essays and Studies on English Language and Literature, VI (Cambridge, Mass./Copenhagen, 1950), p. 158.
30* Holweck, p. 22; and see Réau, 595.
31* Edmond Malone, The Plays and Poems of William Shakespeare (London, 1821; reis. New York, 1966), XVII, 94, n. 3; T. F. Thiselton Dyer, Folk-Lore of Shakespeare (1883; reis. New York, 1966), p. 205.
32* Wilkes, 334-336; see Prometheus, Encyclopedia Britannica, 14th ed. (1929).
33* Sir James G. Frazer, The Golden Bough, 3rd ed. (London, 1911), II, 260; Wilkes, 334-336.
34* M. Grieve, A Modern Herbal (London/New York, 1967), I, 293.
35* See G. Paris' discussion of this legend in his introduction to

Guillaume de Berneville's twelfth century poem, La Vie de saint Gilles, SATF, I (Paris, 1881). See also: Réau, 593-594; The South English Legendary, eds. Charlotte d'Evelyn and Anna J. Mill, EETS 236 (London, 1956), p. 236.

36* See the Parson's Tale, and W. Nelson Francis' edition of The Book of Vices and Virtues, EETS 217 (London, 1942), p. 45.

37* Jung, pp. 313-319, esp. p. 317.

38* For example, The 'Liber de Diversis Medicinis', ed. M. S. Ogden, EETS 207, (London, 1938), p. 10. See also n. 33 (above) for exposure to Midsummer's Eve fires, as cure for eye diseases.

39* Bruce Rosenberg, "The Contrary Tales of the Second Nun and the Canon's Yeoman," Chaucer Review, II (1968), 282-283, 284-285.

40* John Read, The Alchemist in Life, Literature and Art (London, 1947), p. 13.

41* Adolf Katzenellenbogen, Allegories of the Vices and Virtues (New York, 1964), p. 58.

4

THE ST. LOY OATH RECONSIDERED

Much concerning Chaucer's Prioress is enigmatic. Not only is her tale unconquered, as a title of Alan Gaylord's suggests, 1* but, despite the wealth of scholarly effort directed toward it, the Prioress's St. Loy oath has never received a wholly satisfying explanation either. The phrase "diverting byways," which appears in one of Gaylord's footnotes, 2* offers a clue. The oath should not lead away from the text; rather, it should provide a way into it. Such concrete references as this oath are valuable guidelines by which to check the course of interpretations, not diversions to distract the reader's attention.

Courtliness is the theme of the Prioress's General Prologue portrait (A 118-162). 3* The first part of the passage (A 118-141) is an external description of behavior, dealing with overt courtliness - explicit, easily observable signs, such as table manners and speech. In the second part (A 142-150), the description concerns the Prioress's spiritual condition, her conscience, and the theme of courtliness continues, though it is now covert and implicit. Finally, part three (A 151-162) is a description of the Prioress's appearance and the values here, too, are courtly ones. The reference to St. Loy provides some of the thematic continuity between the three parts.

Lowes, in his now famous article on the oath, described and printed excerpts from a medieval French poem, wherein St. Eligius is treated as a romance hero in the best courtly tradition. 4* His appearance and his courtesy are unexcelled, and the court to which he belongs is no less than that of the Blessed Virgin herself. St. Loy is the master of heavenly ceremonies, he gives the archangels their cue to sing, and serves as Our Lady's cupbearer. If he has commended himself to Mary, surely the Prioress would find him attractive. Later Benjamin Wainwright, using Lowes' article as a basis, accurately described the Prioress's emotions for St. Loy. 5* Unfortunately, however, he weakened his observations by adding an apologia, so typical of Prioress critics, declaring he meant no "disrespect," as if he feared legal repercussions from a living person. 6*

In subsequent scholarship on the oath emphasis began to shift from St. Loy himself to his relationships with contemporary religious women. Gordon H. Gerould commented on the saint's having founded several nunneries, though the sparse statement was unexpanded. 7* John M. Steadman broke new ground as he specifically treated one of St. Loy's religious protegés, St. Godeberta. 8* Unfortunately, he limited himself to the one figure, feeling, perhaps, that Madame Eglantine's attraction to the legend would be a one-to-one identification with a specific woman in it. But St. Loy was not only, as Steadman stated,

"spiritual mentor of a Benedictine abbess." 9* He played the lead in
a romance of many episodes, and a reader of his ecclesiastically
correct 'aventure' could identify with several saintly heroines.

In addition to St. Godeberta, already discussed by Steadman, there
are at least three other ladies of the St. Loy salon whom the Prioress
would have found socially correct, morally inspiring and totally romantic. They are all Benedictines, all are saints, and all are connected
with the court - one as its queen, one the daughter of a courtier, and
one a protegé of the courtier St. Loy. Not only are they figures whom
we can imagine the Prioress would find attractive, but their attributes,
appearing throughout the General Prologue passage concerning the
Prioress, substantiate the supposition. It is necessary to examine
the description closely, since here, indeed, "every stroke tells;
every concrete detail carries with it an aura of associations." 10*

The most socially prominent member of St. Loy's circle was the
royal St. Bathilda, wife of King Clovis II of Neustria and Burgundy and
mother of three kings. 11* The romance of Bathilda's legend rivals
that of any secular medieval tale. The young Anglo-Saxon girl was
stolen by pirates, sold as a slave into the household of the mayor of
Clovis' palace, and, because of her beauty and prudence, chosen by
the king as his queen. After the death of her husband, Queen Bathilda
acted as regent until her son Clotaire, whose court included St. Loy,
came to the throne. As regent, with the aid of such courtiers as St.
Loy, she was active in suppressing the slave trade, of which she had
been a victim. Steadman (p. 54) makes the valid point that such charitable acts of Loy's legend - and Bathilda's works strengthen Loy's
still more - heighten the irony of the Prioress's superficial charities
(A 142-150), especially toward the mice caught in traps. Further,
Bathilda's reputation for charity was so great that she was frequently
depicted distributing alms, and was represented by the attribute of
bread. This symbol of St. Bathilda's charity contrasts ironically with
the "wastel-breed" which the Prioress distributes as dog food. And
the irony continues when Bathilda's special patronage of children is
juxtaposed with the Prioress's particular charity to dogs and mice.

The representations of St. Bathilda would be appealing to someone
combining religious aspirations and a love of material elegance. The
saint is shown wearing a crown, sometimes in religious garb, and
standing in the presence of the Virgin of Christ Crucified. The Prioress
would especially appreciate the royal St. Bathilda's attribute of gold,
the material of her brooch and the epitome of luxury, though ironically
in connection with saints it is usually the symbol of alms.

Like Madame Eglantine, Bathilda loved jewels and expensive clothing
and wore them even in her widowhood. According to the official life
of St. Loy, for whom Bathilda's veneration was boundless, the saint
appeared after death in a vision seen by one of his courtiers, ordering
the man to admonish the queen for this practice. The queen immediately
set the garments aside, distributing some of them to the poor, and had
made for St. Loy's tomb a cross encrusted with precious stones from
her jewelry.

St. Bathilda's devotion to the holy man who had been her trusted adviser is illustrated by the anecdote of her rushing to Noyon with her

three sons as Loy lay dying, hoping to receive a final blessing from him. She arrived too late and her only consolation for her loss was uncovering the dead prelate and kissing his face. At the funeral she accompanied his cortege on foot, refusing the comfort of a mount. 12*

Bathilda would also appeal to the Prioress because she was a patron saint of abbesses. She had supported the efforts of a number of religious courtiers including Loy in founding and overseeing religious houses, and she is probably best known as the founder of Corbie and for endowing the nunnery of Chelles, where she retired after her regency. But her life at Chelles was not that of an abbess; she adopted the role of a humble working nun. Her performance of the most menial chores earned her the decidedly uncourtly attribute of a broom. The scullery duties of the queen, elbow-deep in a scrubbing pail, wielding a broom, or washing other people's dirty dishes, contrast sharply with the pretty manners of the Prioress, who did not like to moisten her fingers with her own food (A 129), was careful of the crumbs (A 130-131), and fastidiously wiped away every trace of grease from her lips before picking up her cup (A 134-135). Despite the lowly broom, St. Bathilda is represented in two aristocratic fourteenth century breviaries of famous people, Philippe le Bel and Charles V. 13*

The saint with the most widespread and enduring reputation among St. Loy's acquaintances is Gertrude of Nivelles (Brabant). 14* Her veneration, which was immediate following her death, is shown by the numerous church dedications to her in Brabant and Hainault. She was the daughter of Pepin of Landen, mayor of the palace of King Dagobert, whose court included St. Loy. Gertrude's family was especially devout: her mother was St. Ida and her sister was the matron St. Begga, daughter-in-law of St. Arnulf and grandmother of Charles Martel. When the beautiful Gertrude was a mere child, she refused the marriage proposal of a courtier whose suit the king himself undertook. She declined adamantly, declaring her intention to espouse only the Lord Jesus Christ. Years later, following Pepin's death, her mother built Nivelles, of which Gertrude became the first abbess. Legend has it that St. Ida shaved her daughter's golden hair in the shape of a cross, in order to discourage suitors while the abbey was under construction. She was a religious heroine of such beauty, charm and courtly connections, and whose marriage to the religious life was so romantic, that her potential appeal for the Prioress seems certain.

As it will readily be seen, St. Gertrude's espousal legend has affinities with that of St. Godeberta, discussed by Steadman. In this connection Gertrude wrote, " 'adversity is the ring with which the soul is betrothed to God,' " which is reminiscent of the attribute of Godeberta, the ring, frequently shown being presented to her by St. Loy. Further, St. Gertrude has in common with St. Loy and St. Bathilda a reputation for her charity, which earned her the attribute of a loaf of bread, again suggesting the fine bread which the Prioress fed her "smale houndes."

Gertrude's austerity concerning her personal adornment was so great that she refused even woollen or linen burial sheets, preferring to be interred in the hair shirt she had long worn and a shabby, hand-me-down veil, though the monastery of which she had been head was

so rich in the tenth century that it was reputed to have had 14, 000
families as vassals. 15* St. Gertrude's ragged garb is in ironic contrast
to that of the Prioress, whose wimple "ful semyly ... pynched was"
and whose cloak was "ful fetys. "

Gertrude was a patron saint of travellers and pilgrims, and in connection with this role the expression "Gertruds Minne, " or "Gertruden-
minne, " evolved. Minne, Ger. 'love,' suggests the Amor of the
Prioress's brooch, included in the motto Amor vincit omnia (A 162).
From her patronage of travellers and pilgrims on earth arose her
patronage of souls after death. It is this latter function which has
generated one of the most curious attributes of any Christian saint,
and that by which Gertrude is invariably identified, rats or mice. At
times she is shown holding a single rodent in her hand and again she
is covered with them from head to foot. The rats and mice, which
are omnipresent in Gertrude's representations, immediately suggest
the mouse caught in a trap in the description of the Prioress. 16*

St. Aurea, another spiritual ward of St. Loy, was a Benedictine
abbess, 17* as were Godeberta and Gertrude. (Bathilda, it will be
recalled, was the benefactor of several Benedictine houses, but was
only a simple nun with no administrative duties.) A Syrian by birth,
she came to France after the death of her Christian parents. Her
piety was soon recognized by the religious courtiers, and St. Loy,
who had just founded St. Martial, placed her at the head of the monastery,
where she remained the rest of her life. Play on 'gold,' involving both
the word aurea and the goldsmithing of St. Loy, must have been involved in the medieval nickname of Orfaivresse, by which St. Aurea
was distinguished from the several other saints of the same name. 18*
The appeal of this name for the Lady Prioress with her love of gold
would be considerable.

In addition to the play on 'gold' and goldsmithing, there may be
appropriateness for the General Prologue passage in St. Aurea's life-
long penance, the attribute of which is a nail. The nail alludes to the
chair of nails on which Aurea sat, mortifying her flesh while daily
reciting the 150 psalms, in compensation for her loss of patience
with a poor reading of the Gospel by a deacon. She had seized the
book and read the service herself, so great was her outrage. This
incident recalls the lines in the Prologue beginning, "Ful weel she
soong the service dyvyne" (122f.).

In common with the legends of Sts. Gertrude and Bathilda, Aurea's
legend also includes a crown. An angel was supposed to have placed
a resplendent crown on the saint's head. And Aurea, too, was renowned for her works of mercy, two miracles toward the handicapped
earning her the patronage of those paralyzed and blinded. Like the
crowns of the other two saints, Aurea's symbolized an inner spiritual
nobility, rather than an outer material manifestation of it. In fact, her
austerities were so severe that a sister at the monastery was led to
say, " 'la bouche luy vint torse.' " 19* Aurea's mouth, with which
she fasted, suggests a contrast with the Prioress's "mouth ful smal,
and therto softe and reed, " the ingestion of food through which en-
abled her to display so many of her carefully practiced table manners
(A 127-136).

Aurea was a popular saint in France, being the second patron of Paris after St. Genevieve. Her most important link to the life of St. Loy was in his foretelling her death. Loy, who had been dead for a year, appeared in a vision to a young man he had known when alive, bidding the man to tell St. Aurea that her death was imminent and that she should come to him.

All the members of the St. Loy religious salon who have been discussed are worthy of Madame Eglantine's attention. The gold of their crowns and glitter of their courtly acquaintances constitute the epitome of social success: they were 'of the court,' and they were protegés of one of the most romantic religious figures, St. Loy. The Prioress's vicarious participation in their circle, via church approved literature, is not difficult to imagine. But these saints' consistent pattern of gold-crowns-nobility is just as consistently counterbalanced by bread-austerities-charity. The aristocratic behavior of these women stands in monumental contrast to the Prioress's proper table manners, fastidious garb and tears for bleeding mice and beaten dogs, creatures who happened to be present at her feet. St. Loy's ladies shunned worldliness in dress and manners, but administered charities to alleviate real human miseries, which they sought out in a very real world.

The ramifications of an oath by St. Loy are many indeed. It is easily the "gretteste ooth" of the Canterbury Tales. Far from diverting attention from the General Prologue, the attributes and allusions to all the personae of St. Loy's legend constitute a sort of iconographic acrostic inextricably worked into the passage. Nor is the comment on the Prioress's courtliness restricted to the General Prologue: the satire extends to the Friar's Tale, where the saint "très aristocratique" invoked by the courtly nun is juxtaposed with the saint "très démocratique" invoked by the carter (D 1564). And, of course, the more we learn of the Prioress in the Prologue, the greater the comment on her role as teller of the Prioress's Tale. Most importantly, however, the oath by St. Loy informs Chaucer's concept of courtesy throughout the Tales. The Prioress "peyned hire to countrefete cheere/ Of court ... And to ben holden digne of reverence," not realizing that "unto vertu longeth dignitee, / And noght the revers, .../ Al were he mytre, croune, or diademe" (Gentilesse, 5-7).

NOTES

1* Alan T. Gaylord, "The Unconquered Tale of the Prioress," Papers of the Michigan Academy of Science, Arts and Letters, XLVII (1962), 613-636.

2* Ibid., 618, n.15.

3* All references are to The Works of Geoffrey Chaucer, ed. F. N. Robinson, 2nd ed. (Cambridge, Mass., 1957).

4* John L. Lowes, "The Prioress's Oath," Romanic Review, V (1914), 376f.

5* Benjamin B. Wainwright, "Chaucer's Prioress Again: An Interpretative Note," Modern Language Notes, XLVIII (1933), 34-37.

6* This whole phenomenon is curious. It is as if the critics expected the wrath of the Church 600 years retroactively, or that the formidable woman herself were confronting them at lectern or typewriter. To adopt what Gaylord calls a "hard" interpretation is to invite the disdain of many Chaucerians, who, in good medieval fashion, champion the cause of the Lady Prioress, for whom they imagine Chaucer had some special affection. See E. Talbot Donaldson, Speaking of Chaucer (New York, 1970), p. 3f.

7* Gordon H. Gerould, Chaucerian Essays (New York, 1951), p. 16.

8* John M. Steadman, " 'Hir Gretteste Ooth': The Prioress, St. Eligius, and St. Godebertha, " Neophilologus, XLIII (1959), 49-57.

9* Ibid., 54, 57.

10* Lowes, 368.

11* Information concerning the life of St. Bathilda may be found in the Acta Sanctorum [AASS], 26 January, and in the sources listed by Louis Réau, Iconographie de l'art Chrétien, III (Paris, 1958-1959), 187-188, and in Butler's Lives of the Saints, eds. Herbert Thurston and Donald Attwater (New York, 1956), I, 204-205. For information concerning her legend and iconography see also: J. Corblet, Hagiographie du diocese d'Amiens, IV (Paris/Amiens, 1874), 172-175, III (1873), 520, II (1870), 268; F. G. Holweck, A Biographical Dictionary of the Saints (St. Louis, 1924), p. 142; Agnes B. C. Dunbar, A Dictionary of Saintly Women (London, 1904), I, 105-106; Helen Roeder, Saints and Their Attributes (Chicago, 1956), p. 357; Karl Künstle, Ikonographie der Heiligen (Freiburg-im-Breisgau, 1926), p. 121; and Otto Wimmer, Handbuch der Namen und Heiligen (Innsbruck/Wien/München, 1953), pp. 135-136.

12* Dunbar, I, 106.

13* Réau, III, 188.

14* AASS, 21 February, and in St. Ultan's life, 1 May; Corblet, IV, 302, and III, 584-585; Bibliotheca Sanctorum, Pontificia università Lateranense, VI (Rome, 1965), cols. 288-291; Réau, III, 586-587; Dunbar, I, 342-345; Künstle, pp. 280-281; Wimmer, pp. 228-229; Holweck, p. 432; and Roeder, p. 351.

15* Dunbar, I, 344.

16* Réau, III, 587, n. 2, for example, mentions the symbolism of St. Gertrude's mice. It has been observed that the Prioress could feel pity for a mouse caught in a trap, although she could dispassionately relate the killing of fellow human beings whose only sin was their Jewishness. The irony doubles when we discover that mice sometimes symbolized Jews. See Joshua Trachtenberg, The Devil and the Jews (New Haven, 1943), p. 86, and the comment by George Ferguson, Signs and Symbols in Christian Art (New York, 1966), p. 24, on the "evil" connotation of the mouse symbol in general.

17* AASS, 4 October:; Bibliotheca Sanctorum, II (1962), cols. 596-599; Dunbar, I, 92f.; Corblet, IV, 166; Réau, III, 158.

18* Corblet, IV, 166.

19* Réau, III, 158.

5

HENDE OLD ST. NICHOLAS IN THE MILLER'S TALE*

Saints have always provided a fertile source of names, and since
Nicholas was one of the most popular saints in the entire Christian
canon, his legend is a reasonable place to direct one's curiosity concerning Chaucer's name choice for the Miller's clerk. The legend of
St. Nicholas of Myra, later of Bari, familiar to both eastern and western Christendom, 1* was included in the Golden Legend, 2* and his
feast, December sixth, with its election of the Boy Bishop in many
localities, 3* would have impressed itself on the Christian's memory
early in childhood. St. Nicholas' popularity is further attested by the
fact that there were over 500 Latin hymns composed and sung in his
honor and more than 400 ancient church dedications for him in England alone. 4* The details of this saint's legend are so well documented
in ecclesiastical art - Chartres alone has seven representations of
Nicholas - that Chaucer's audience from the humblest upward would
certainly have recognized them. 5*
    It is not difficult to discover the probable reason for Chaucer's
choice of name for the hende clerk: Nicholas was the patron saint of
clerks. 6* Of the many legends of Nicholas, the one which probably
connected him with the clerks is essentially as follows:

> Three clerks came to an inn, asking for a night's lodging. While
> they slept, they were murdered by the innkeeper and his wife. Soon
> after, St. Nicholas also came to the inn, where he requested fresh
> meat. At the innkeeper's declaration that he had none, the saint
> revealed his knowledge of the murdered clerks, the innkeeper and
> his wife repented, and the three clerks were resuscitated. 7*

Wace's Vie de Saint Nicholas, containing an economic version of this
legend, includes a few lines on the clerks' celebration of St. Nicholas:

> Por ceo que as clers fist tiel honor,
> Font li clerc feste a icel jor
> De bien lirre, de bien chantier,
> E de miracles recitier. 8*

The legend of St. Nicholas is so rich and the tale of the Miller so intriguing, it is difficult to believe Chaucer's sense of satire let him
develop the allusion to this saint no further than the facile stage of
occupational aptness. Beyond the easy name choice for a clerk, the
similarity between Nicholas the saint and Nicholas the clerk is clearly
satiric. We learn from the Golden Legend that the saint "passait ses

* Some of the material in chapters 5 - 7 was included in a paper on
Chaucerian allusion given at the Conference on Chaucer, November,
1973, State University of New York at Albany.

nuits en prières, macérait son corps, fuyait la société des femmes," 9*
for example. The contrast with the Miller's Nicholas is monumental.
Not only are the characters of the two Nicholases themselves comparable satirically, but the host-guest relationships in which they are
involved invite comparison as well. The relationship of John, the
"riche gnof, that gestes heeld to bord" (A 3188) in his "hostelrye"
(A 3203) and his boarder is an inversion of the relationship between
the innkeeper and the clerks in the above legend of the saint. 10* In
the legend, although the host's malice is directed toward the innocent
clerks, ultimately all are redeemed, the innkeeper and his wife from
sin and the clerks from death. In Chaucer's tale, the landlord is the
recipient of the malice, the clerk is the donor, and both are finally
punished. Nicholas has a burned "towte" (A 3853), Alisoun is "swyved"
(A 3850), and John "was holde wood in al the toun" (A 3846).

After the statement of how "this clerk was cleped" (A 3199), the
tale contains a description of Nicholas and his room. We learn that
the chamber was "Ful fetisly ydight with herbes swoote;/ And he hymself
[was] as sweete as is the roote/ Of lycorys, or any cetewale" (A 3205-
3207). Further, in A 3219, he is referred to as "this sweete clerk. "
That the clerk should emit such sweetness and that his dwelling should
likewise be perfumed is especially fitting for a namesake of St. Nicholas.
One of the traditional stories of the saint is the miracle of the sweet
oil, the "Manna of St. Nicholas, " that issued from his tomb in Bari
and, in some variations, of the sweetness that emanated from the body
itself. 11* This legend probably evolved through a pun on _Myre_, of
which the saint was said to be "pontife le Myre oint par la myrrhe
divine. " 12* Nevertheless, a medieval pilgrimage to Bari evolved
because of the manna of the tomb and its purported cures, 13* and
there seems no doubt that the story was accepted literally. As a result of this phase of the Nicholas legend, he is the patron saint of
perfumers. 14*

That the clerk is specifically represented as singing _Angelus ad_
virginem (A 3216) is particularly interesting with respect to the St.
Nicholas legend. This is a hymn on the Annunciation, 15* celebrated
at Salisbury during the second week after the feast of St. Nicholas,
during the tenure of the Boy Bishop, or Nicholas Bishop as he was
sometimes called. 16* St. Nicholas is frequently connected with the
worship of the Virgin Mary, partly because of his general reputation
as a saint of charity, but more specifically because of a legend of
intervention by the Virgin and Christ on behalf of the saint at the Coun-
cil of Nicea in 321. 17* Nicholas is frequently found with Mary in
ecclesiastical art, sometimes as her attendant. 18* The connection
between the Blessed Virgin and St. Nicholas may have been reinforced
by calendar, art and sermon as well. An invocation of the saint immediately after that of Mary is found in a twelfth century sermon by Peter
Damian. 19* A satiric implication of the charitable aspect of the Nicholas
legend is also present in the Miller's Tale (A 3219-3220): "this sweete
clerk his tyme spente/ After his freendes fyndyng and his rente. " St.
Nicholas is represented in his legends and iconography as, above all,
charitable, the ready benefactor to the needy. Nicholas the clerk,
however, is not the donor but the recipient of charity, living off the

generosity of his friends.

Following the description of the clerk, the Miller's Tale includes a portrait of Alisoun, a bride (A 3221), only eighteen years old (A 3223). Once again the material recalls St. Nicholas. This saint is the patron of brides and young girls, especially of the bourgeoisie, such as Alisoun, fitting "For any lord to leggen in his bedde, / Or yet for any good yeman to wedde" (A 3269-3270). 20* These patronages were earned through the very popular legend of the three maidens, referred to variously as the "Charity of St. Nicholas, " the "Dowry, " or Tres Filiae. The salient points of the story are as follows:

> A father who had fallen into financial difficulties was faced with the choice of prostitution or starvation for his three young daughters, since he could not provide for them elsewise. The good St. Nicholas, hearing of their plight, anonymously donated dowries to the girls on three successive nights by tossing bags of gold coins through their window. 21*

This legend is contained in the literary references to the saint, as well as having wide circulation in the graphic arts and in drama. 22* Alisoun's portrait contains the specific icons of the dowry legend of St. Nicholas. In A 3250 there is mentioned "a purs of lether. " The purse is one of the most frequently encountered symbols for Nicholas and is usually seen in a group of three, either as actual purses or, as they e-volved, gold balls, eventually adopted as the sign of the pawnbroker. 23* Another hint of the dowry legend is Chaucer's use of gold coins in his description of Alisoun: "brighter was the shynyng of hir hewe/ Than in the Tour the noble yforged newe" (A 3255-3256). And another possible implication of the legend, with its anonymous donor, is that Nicholas, clerk, "Of deerne love ... koude and of solas;/ And therto he was sleigh and ful privee" (A 3200-3201). This may be a satiric echo of St. Nicholas' life, since the holy man was loathe to expose his generosity, preferring to bestow his gifts unobtrusively. The father of the three young women in the story had to lie in wait, ready to seize the benefactor, since the young saint had failed to stop when simply called. 24*

Alisoun's portrait contains other reminders of St. Nicholas. The legend of the sweet manna is recalled with A 3261: "Hir mouth was sweete as bragot or the meeth. " And the line following contains still another Nicholas icon, apples, the symbol of fruit evolving from the golden balls as more appropriate for the saint in his role as Father Christmas. 25*

Almost all of the legends of St. Nicholas fall into one of two cate-gories, those which are variations on the rescue or resuscitation of three people or those which concern the sea. With A 3264 there begins the accumulation of allusions to the latter type: the young bride is de-scribed as "Long as a mast. " The nautical motif increases further on as the discussion of the imminent flood and the preparations for it proceed (A 3516f.). St. Nicholas is especially well known as the patron saint of sailors and was evoked by sea travellers against tempest and general calamity at sea. 26* The legend from which these patronages

arose is found in several variations, but the salient aspects are the
same in all of them: St. Nicholas, on his way to the Holy Land by ship,
was entreated to save the crew when a tempest arose. He banished
the storm and saved the ship. Later a sailor drowned and was restored
to life by the saint. 27* Nicholas is frequently represented with the
icons of ship or anchor because of this part of his legend. 28* Attributed
to Joinville is the anecdote of the queen who, when involved in a storm
on the Mediterranean in 1254, promised St. Nicholas a ship of silver
in return for her safety. 29* The sea legend is applicable to the Miller's
Tale in still another aspect: as John the carpenter follows Nicholas'
instructions, he becomes a shipwright, and thus the saint's patronage
of shipbuilders is appropriate for him. 30*

In the description of Absolon, too, there are reminders of the Nicholas legend, satiric though they may be. The allusion to sweetness is
again evident. There is the statement that Absolon swings the censer,
perfuming the parish wives on holy days (A 3340-3341). And his gifts
to Alisoun include sweet drinks, mentioned in A 3378, recalling Nicholas' several patronages in the wine industry. 31* Lines A 3352f. recall
the vignette of the three maidens, so often represented in art, with St.
Nicholas as a young man, standing on tiptoe in the full of the moon
under the young girls' bedroom window, the father in the background,
looking quite unhappy. 32* Absolon stands in the full of the moon under
the window of Alisoun's room, in which there is also a chagrined, old
man, her husband. Absolon's gifts (A 3379-3380) include more St.
Nicholas icons and images: wine, wafers and money. The food suggests
the gifts of the Christmas tradition, the saint's icon of bread, 33* his
patronage of the wine industry, and the money is, again, suggestive
of the doweries.

There are additional St. Nicholas allusions used in connection with
Absolon further on in the tale. Again the sweetness is stressed (A
3690-3692): "he cheweth greyn and lycorys, / To smellen sweete, er
he hadde kembed his heer. / Under his tonge a trewe-love he beer. "
A bit further he calls Alisoun "hony-comb, sweete Alisoun, ... my
sweete cynamome" (A 3698-3699). Again there is a window scene
(A 3695 f.) and, also once more, the imagery is reminiscent of the
icons of the St. Nicholas legend as represented in art: gold (A 3779),
a bag full of coins (A 3780), and a golden ring (A 3794). The scene
is an ironic inversion of the ecclesiastical representation, with Absolon's goal not protection from, but invitation to, the young woman's
"swyvening. "

The culmination of the third window scene, at the tale's end, is not
only a neat binding up of Chaucer's two episodes, but a juncture for
the combination of the two main St. Nicholas legends. In addition to
the dowry legend the scene is a reminder of the saint's invocation
against tempest and catastrophe at sea, with the repetitive "water,
water" (A 3815, 3817). Further, Nicholas' burned "toute" (A 3810 f.)
recalls the saint's invocation against fire, earned by his restoration to
health of a burned child, by making the sign of the cross above it. 34*
It also suggests the story of Nicholas' having thwarted a scheme
to burn the church in Bari in which his relics are contained by per-
suading pilgrims, victims of Satanic demons, that the oil with which

they planned to anoint the church was an incendiary agent. 35* And in connection with the burning of Nicholas' "towte" and the St. Nicholas legend, it is interesting to wonder if the old Rumanian tradition of putting the bad children's hands to St. Nicholas' coals "pour leur donner une idee plus saisissante de l'enfer dont il les menace" 36* could be old enough for Chaucer to have known.

A further reminder of the Christmas tradition and St. Nicholas occurs at the end of the Miller's Tale. There are two references not to Noe's, but to Nowelis flood (A 3818, 3834). This suggests the saint in his role as Father Christmas, the gist of "Nowelis flood" being "Nicholas' flood."

In addition to the images or situations in the Miller's Tale which are, either straightforwardly or satirically, comparable to the St. Nicholas legends, there are fleeting images which in themselves are slight but which, taken together, form an appropriate backdrop for the more obvious parallels. For example, the mention of Satan (A 3750) and the following references to the forge (A 3762), hot coulter and fire-place (A 3776), suggestive of the devil, are reminiscent of some of the literary and graphic representations of St. Nicholas. In depicting a legend of butchered children served up as meat for humans (and ultimately restored to life by Nicholas), artists presented the murderer as the devil, 37* and in a number of his written legends Nicholas contends with the devil. 38* Immediately following these diabolic references, and within the same scene - that of the blacksmith shop - are the more familiar St. Nicholas icons of gold (A 3779) and a bag of coins (A 3780).

Another suggestion of the St. Nicholas legend occurs in A 3463. The carpenter, worrying about the clerk's long stay in his room, says of Nicholas, "He shal be rated of his studying." St. Nicholas, the patron saint of scholars and school boys, "was distinguished ... for his gravity and his attention to his studies." 39* Still another legend of St. Nicholas credits the saint with rescuing three erroneously accused prisoners only moments before their death. 40* For this feat he is a patron saint of prisoners and, at least with tongue in cheek, appropriate for both Alisoun and John. In the description of the young wife, we find, concerning the carpenter, "Jalous he was, and heeld hire narwe in cage" (A 3224), and, seven lines further, we realize that the husband is also a captive, since "he was fallen in the snare" of marriage to a much younger woman. The provisioning of Nicholas for his stay of a day or two in his chamber (A 3410-3411) and John's procurement of "vitaille" for the tubs for a day or so (A 3627-3629), recall that St. Nicholas' legends include at least two incidents of fast and famine. Nicholas' piety prompted him to fast, even as an infant, when on Wednesdays and Fridays he took his mother's milk only once a day. 41* And there is a story of St. Nicholas' provisioning of the masses during a famine by multiplying wheat. 42* The icon of bread, appropriate to this St. Nicholas legend, is found in 1. 3628.

And, finally, figuring frequently in the background of the Miller's Tale, is the motif of the chiffre sacré, three, which is present in so many of the St. Nicholas legends. 43* In the tale there are the obvious threes: three men, three window scenes, three tubs, and three ladders. And there is the less evident, but no less important, theme of the three sins omnipresent in the tale. 44*

More signal than all the other allusions to St. Nicholas in the Miller's Tale, however, is that which occurs in A 3636-3637. Alisoun, John and Nicholas, sitting in their three vats, present a scene highly suggestive of the most popular of the St. Nicholas icons, the three men in tubs. Though the three-men-in-a-tub representation, with its nursery rhyme tone, is quite frequent, the three figures in three individual tubs may also be encountered in the iconography of St. Nicholas. (For instance, there is an excellent late fourteenth century example of St. Nicholas with three figures in separate tubs by Gentile da Fabriano.) 45* This icon, probably influenced by the three boys resuscitated from pickling tubs, or possibly by the legend of the pious infant St. Nicholas standing to praise God in his bathtub, in all likelihood evolved from the legend of the three falsely accused men, or the legend of the three clerks. 46* Nevertheless, the scene of the three naked figures, wearing only pious expressions, rising from tubs around the elegant bishop-saint, must have been evoked in the minds of the medieval audience by the comically parallel scene of the tub trio in the Miller's Tale, wearing their expressions of fatigue and adultery.

NOTES

1* Mary S. Crawford, Life of St. Nicholas (Philadelphia, 1923), pp. 9-12; Louis Réau, Iconographie de l'art Chrétien, III, Pt. 2 (Paris, 1958), 976-988; Jules Laroche, Vie de Saint Nicolas (Paris, 1886); Anna B. Jameson, Sacred and Legendary Art (Boston, 1896), I, 57-71; Bibliotheca Sanctorum, IX (Rome, 1967), 923-947.
2* Jacques de Voragine, La Légende Dorée (Paris, 1843), I, 41-47. N. B., I have used the French version since Chaucer must have read that language as easily as English and because the French translation is more nearly contemporary with his own lifetime than the Latin original.
3* Karl Young, The Drama of the Medieval Church (Oxford, 1933), I, 106.
4* Crawford, p. 12; Francis Bond, Dedications of English Churches (London, 1914), p. 237.
5* Réau, 980-988; Émile Mâle, Religious Art in France in the Thirteenth Century, trans. Dora Nussey, 3rd ed. (New York/London, 1913), pp. 328-330; Alban Butler, Lives of the Saints, eds. Herbert Thurston and Donald Attwater (New York, 1956), IV, 506.
6* The Reader's Encyclopedia, ed. William Rose Benét (New York, 1955), pp. 975, 981; Young, II, 329, 490.
7* Young, II, 324-337.
8* Young, II, 328; La Vie de Saint Nicolas par Wace ... publié d'après tous les Manuscrits, ed. Einar Ronsjö (Lund, 1942), p. 122.
9* Légende Dorée, 42.
10* Citations are from The Works of Geoffrey Chaucer, ed. F. N. Robinson, 2nd ed. (Cambridge, Mass., 1957).
11* Mâle, p. 329; Réau, 977-978, 979.

12* Réau, 979, n. 3.
13* Young, II, 308-309. The South Porch of Chartres shows St. Nicholas' tomb and some ailing pilgrims who have come to be cured by the miraculous liquid oozing from it.
14* Réau, 979.
15* Robinson, p. 684.
16* Young, I, 106; II, 245; E. K. Chambers, The Mediaeval Stage (Oxford, 1903), I, 336-371.
17* Sabine Baring-Gould, Lives of the Saints (Edinburgh, 1914), XV, 66-67; Laroche, p. 88f.
18* Anna B. Jameson, Legends of the Madonna, 2nd ed. (Boston, 1857) pp. 100, 105, 182, 184, 192, 200, 245.
19* Mâle, p. 329; Crawford, p. 12: "[St. Nicholas] is in the religious lore, the counterpart of the Virgin, his fame even having priority in point of time over hers ... The deeds of St. Nicholas help the needy in all strata of society. As the Virgin is the celestial Mother of humanity, the world-helper, so St. Nicholas is the earthly friend of those in distress. "
20* Jameson, Sac. and Leg. Art, 57; Reader's Enc. , p. 980.
21* Réau, 982-983; Légende Dorée, 41-42.
22* Young, II, 311-324, 488-490. This episode is shown both on the South Porch and in stained glass at Chartres.
23* R. L. P. Milburn, Saints and Their Emblems in English Churches (Oxford, 1961), p. 191; H. P. Brewster, Saints and Festivals of the Christian Church (New York, 1904), p. 13.
24* Légende Dorée, 42; Young, II, 314-315, 322.
25* Bond, pp. 325, 298; Réau, 980.
26* Réau, 979.
27* Légende Dorée, 42; Jameson, Sac. and Leg. Art, 60, 63, 68.
28* Bond, p. 325; Otto Wimmer, Handbuch der Namen und Heiligen (Innsbruck/Wien/München, 1953), p. 370.
29* Mâle, p. 329.
30* Réau, 979.
31* Ibid.
32* A. N. Didron, Christian Iconography, tr. Margaret Stokes (London, 1891), II, 368; Jameson, Sac. and Leg. Art, 59-60.
33* Wimmer, p. 369.
34* Baring-Gould, 65.
35* Légende Dorée, 43; Réau, 987.
36* Laroche, p. 360.
37* Jameson, Sac. and Leg. Art, 61, 65.
38* Laroche, for example, p. 62.
39* Jameson, Sac. and Leg. Art, 59.
40* Légende Dorée, 43-44; Réau, 983-984, 980.
41* Légende Dorée, 41; Réau, 976, 892.
42* Légende Dorée, 43; Jameson, Sac. and Leg. Art, 60-61.
43* Réau, 977.
44* D. W. Robertson, Jr. , A Preface to Chaucer (Princeton, 1963), p. 382.
45* "San Niccolo Resuscita Tre Fanciulli" by Gentile da Fabriano (b. 1370). Bicci di Lorenzo's representation of the same subject,

along with his painting of the dowry legend, is conveniently available in Allardyce Nicoll's World Drama (New York, 1949), facing p. 161. And see Réau, 980, 984; Bond, pp. 298, 325; Milburn, pp. 190-191.
46* Réau, 977; Laroche, p. 375f.

6

ST. NICHOLAS AND THE PRIORESS'S CALENDAR

The tale told by Chaucer's Lady Prioress is done in ecclesiastical decor to match its teller. Not only is the tale a precise type, a Miracle of the Virgin, tidily placed between an invocation to the Virgin and an historical analogue, but it is neatly set into the church calendar. Within the tale there are a number of references to holy people or events whose celebrations occur so close to one another in the liturgical year that a calendar for the tale may be devised. Marie Hamilton has discussed one event in the festive framework, the Feast of Innocents or Childermas. 1* This occasion comes near the end of a considerably larger liturgical period allotted for the tale, a span covering most of the Christmas season. The little clergeon himself has said that he hopes to learn the Alma redemptoris "er Christemasse be went" (B^2 1730). 2*

In addition to Childermas, the Prioress's Tale, with its Marian invocation and other references to the Virgin, clearly celebrates the Annunciation. In the Western liturgy, particularly the Sarum Use, the Annunciation could be celebrated during the Christmas season - on Wednesday of December Ember Days (i. e., the Wednesday next following December thirteenth). 3* Further, the Alma redemptoris is, it will be recalled, an Advent hymn. 4*

Editors of the Prioress's Tale always point out the lily (B^2 1651) and the burning bush (B^2 1658), as Marian symbols of the Annunciation. The flower is found almost without exception in scenes of the visitation of Gabriel in art, and the burning bush of Moses is, of course, an Old Testament prefiguration of the Immaculate Conception. 5* (Though his assumption was erroneous, Myrc attributed the lily of the traditional Annunciation scene not to symbolism of virginity but to a miracle of the conversion of a Jew, 6* it is interesting to note in connection with the Prioress's Tale.) And Baugh reminds us that the Ave Marie itself (B^2 1698) is "the beginning of a prayer constructed from the words of the Annunciation" (Luke, 1:28, 42). 7*

Though less obvious, there are other allusions to the Virgin, particularly to the Annunciation, found in the tale. Though the Annunciation is the main Marian event commemorated within the Christmas season, the events of the childhood of Christ and episodes of his mother's life were considered a part of this season, as opposed to the other major Christian event, the Resurrection. Hence many incidents of the Virgin's life, seemingly unconnected with Christmas, are found in medieval Nativity representations in graphic art and the drama. 8* The symbol of the serpent (B^2 1748), as sin or Satan, is frequent in sculpture and paintings of Mary. 9* Rachel (B^2 1817), in addition to her connection with the Innocents, is found often in her role as the ideal of the contemplative life, serving as an emblem of the Virgin. 10*

The Prioress's Tale not only contains Annunciation symbols, it is an Annunciation symbol itself. The little Christian boy who, though presumed to be dead, was heard singing within his place of death is, like Moses' burning bush unburnt, symbolic of perpetual chastity. The incident is reminiscent of one of the most popular Old Testament Annunciation stories: just as the Christians whom Nebuchadnezzar threw into the fiery furnace were so filled with the Holy Spirit that they were heard singing in the midst of the fire, "so the Holy Spirit impregnated the Holy Virgin with His inner fire, while without He protected her against all concupiscence." 11* The story of Daniel in the lions' den, frequently cited as a type of the Annunciation, 12* also has affinities with the Prioress's Tale. The Play of Daniel, which includes the lions' den episode and reference to the Nativity, was performed at some time during the Christmas season, probably at either the Feast of Circumcision (January 1) or elsewhere during the Feast of Fools. 13* And the story of Nebuchadnezzar and the fiery furnace, found within the Procession of Prophets, was also performed during the Christmas season. 14*

St. John the Evangelist, also referred to in the Prioress's Tale (B² 1772), is another biblical character connected with the Virgin Mary in art. In representations of the Crucifixion Mary is not only Christ's mother, but is also the personification of the Church, "while St. John, strange as the symbolism may appear to us, represents the Synagogue," 15* an interesting point of contrast in view of the theme of Church triumphant over Synagogue in the tale told by the Prioress.

In addition to the Feast of Innocents (December 28) and the Annunciation (approximately December 14-20), the earliest event in the tale is December 5-6, the Eve and Feast of St. Nicholas (B² 1704). 16* Within this span of December 5-28, the church calendar also includes the Eve of the Nativity and Christmas itself (December 24, 25), St. Stephen's Day (December 26), and the Feast of St. John (December 27), already mentioned. During all of this period of a little more than three weeks, St. Nicholas of Myra is the presiding saint. 17*

The Boy Bishop, often called "Nicholas" (episcopus Nicholatensis), was elected at the first date during the period, that is, December 5-6. 18* Certainly the election of the Boy Bishop and the anticipation of the celebration at which he was to reign were not forgotten by the youthful participants during the interval between election and celebration. A. F. Leach points out that this was the one bright event in the medieval schoolboy's otherwise bleak year. 19* In addition to the importance attached to the date of December 28 by the boys, adults, perhaps in remembrance of their own childhoods, seem to have placed special emphasis on it also: there are records of rich ecclesiastical paraphernalia for the Boy Bishop in medieval church inventories, such as " 'a gold ring with great stone for the Bishop of Innocents' " in fourteenth century York. 20*

The Annunciation, with its emphasis on the expectation of the Holy Child, would have encouraged veneration of St. Nicholas as the patron saint of children. "In the Middle Ages St. Nicholas was not only the protector of children but also the patron of parenthood, the fosterer of family fertility."21* Adriaan DeGroot has noted the "coincidence of the December sixth date and the Teutonic 'period of fertility.' " 22* Proof that the Nativity itself emphasized St. Nicholas' patronage is the saint's role as Father Christmas. He is found in all European countries visiting children sometime between the eve of his feast (December 5) and Epiphany (January 6). 23* As 'Samichlaus' in Switzerland and 'Nicker' in the north of Germany, St. Nicholas was the equivalent of the stork. 24* In fact, in some parts of Europe, "praying to Nicholas" still means 'being pregnant' and the expression "Nicholas has come, " 'the child is born.' 25*

The days following Christmas, with their inverted ecclesiastical hierarchy - Deacons' Day (December 26), Priests' Day (December 27), and the day for choirboys (December 28) 26* - culminated in the day of supremacy for children, when St. Nicholas plays were performed 27* and the Nicholas processions, sometimes quite boisterous in their Halloween-like nature, were staged. 28*

It is interesting to wonder how personally involved in this traditional celebration the Prioress herself might have been in her girlhood, for the nunneries, too, participated in the Feast of Innocents. 29* One record admonishes an abbess that the nuns " 'should not do elsewhere what is done by Holy Virgins on Innocents' Day and let the sacred offices and prayers be offered by girls.' " 30* What is termed "December License" seems to have prevailed during December 16-28 for not only young male ecclesiastics but for their female counterparts as well, since several records show they were rebuked for such things as excessive drinking, frivolities, singing, fraternizing with men, wearing secular clothes and watching performances of plays in which actors " 'provok[ed] voluptuousness among the virgins, with their profane, amorous, and secular gesticulations.' " 31*

The Nicholas Bishop, who reigned at Innocents' Day, was " 'a compound ... represent[ing] a fusion of the Juvenilis of the Saturnalia with the cult of St. Nicholas of Myra.' " 32* The Christmas season brought a bright spot in the darkest part of the year when Mary was worshipped for bringing the Christ Child to the world for its salvation and when, in the name of St. Nicholas, release from earthly sobriety might be had.

St. Nicholas, the "chief mythical figure of the [winter] festival,"33* controls the earthly liturgical activities of this part of the year, while the Blessed Virgin and her Child are celebrated as celestially supreme. St. Mary and St. Nicholas are frequently found together in art. As a saint of charity (from which aspect of his legend the Father Christmas role evolved), 34* St. Nicholas is often seen as an attendant of Mary. 35* His patronage of children and motherhood makes him particularly fitting for his several appearances in Madonna and Child representations.

Dual tribute to the Holy Mother and Nicholas can be found not only in art and literature but also in instances in the liturgy. Peter Damian, in one of his twelfth century sermons, "enjoins the invocation of St. Nicholas immediately after that of the Virgin. He regards him as the most powerful protector whose aid the Christian can invoke. " 36*

Also, the censing of the altar and St. Nicholas' image on St. Nicholas'
Eve were traditionally followed by an anthem to St. Mary. 37*
 If the saints found in the Prioress's Prologue and Tale can be said
to constitute a formal group, a portion of the liturgical calendar, St.
Nicholas is surely its master of ceremonies.

NOTES

1* "Echoes of Childermas in the Tale of the Prioress," Modern
Language Review, XXXIV (1939), 1-8.
2* Chaucer citations are from The Works of Geoffrey Chaucer, ed.
F. N. Robinson, 2nd ed. (Cambridge, Mass.), unless otherwise indicated.
3* Karl Young, The Drama of the Medieval Church (Oxford, 1933),
II, 245; Hardin Craig, English Religious Drama (Oxford, 1955), pp.
61-62.
4* The Works of Geoffrey Chaucer, ed. W. W. Skeat, 2nd ed. (London,
1900), V, 177; Chaucer's Major Poetry, ed. A. C. Baugh (New York,
1963), p. 343, n. to B 1708.
5* Émile Mâle, The Gothic Image, trans. Dora Nussey (New York,
1958), pp. 146, 150, etc.; Anna B. Jameson, Legends of the Madonna,
corr. 2nd ed. (London, 1907), pp. 38-39. For other Annunciation
symbols, see George Ferguson, Signs and Symbols in Christian Art
(New York, 1966).
6* G. G. Coulton, Art and the Reformation (Oxford, 1928), p. 263.
7* Baugh, p. 343, n. to B 1698.
8* Mâle, p. 183; see also Young, II.
9* Jameson, Madonna, p. 40.
10* Ibid., p. 42.
11* Mâle, p. 149.
12* Mâle, p. 149.
13* Young, II, 303; I, 105.
14* Young, II, 168-169.
15* Mâle, pp. 190-191.
16* We are not concerned with the historical facts of St. Nicholas'
life - for there is little known about it - but with the legend, i. e.,
what medieval man knew of Nicholas from art, drama, literature and
folklore. See Butler's Lives of the Saints, eds. Herbert Thurston,
S. J., and Donald Attwater (New York, 1956), IV, 503-506; Sabine
Baring-Gould, Lives of the Saints (London, 1898), XV, 64-68; Bibliotheca Sanctorum, IX (Rome, 1967), 923-947; Jacques de Voragine,
La Légende Dorée (Paris, 1843), I, 41-47; Mary S. Crawford,
Life of St. Nicholas (Philadelphia, 1923); Adriaan D. DeGroot, Saint
Nicholas: A Psychoanalytic Study of His History and Myth (The Hague/
Paris, 1965); Louis Réau, Iconographie de l'art Chrétien, III, Pt. 2
(Paris, 1959), 976-988; Jules Laroche, Vie de saint Nicolas (Paris,
1886); Anna B. Jameson, Sacred and Legendary Art, 8th ed. (London,
1879), II, 450-465.
17* Arthur F. Leach, "The Schoolboys' Feast," Fortnightly Review,
LIX, N. S. (January, 1896), 129.

18* DeGroot, p. 44; Leach, 133; Young, I, 106; see also E. K. Chambers, The Mediaeval Stage (Oxford, 1903), I, 336-371.
19* 129ff.
20* Leach, 132.
21* DeGroot, p. 107.
22* DeGroot, p. 132.
23* DeGroot, p. 19f.
24* DeGroot, p. 131.
25* DeGroot, p. 109.
26* Leach, 131-132; Young, I, 104.
27* Hamilton, in Chaucer: Modern Essays in Criticism, ed. Edward Wagenknecht (New York, 1959), p. 93.
28* Leach, 134; DeGroot, pp. 26ff.
29* Leach, 139-140.
30* Leach, 139.
31* Leach, 139-140.
32* Leach, 141.
33* Chambers, I, 263.
34* Réau, 979.
35* Jameson, Art, 460, 464.
36* Mâle, p. 329.
37* Leach, 133.

7

ST. NICHOLAS AND THE PRIORESS'S "CURSED JEWES"

Though the Prioress in Chaucer's <u>Canterbury Tales</u> refers to St.
Nicholas by name only once, he 'stands ever in one's presence'
throughout her tale. His connection with the Feast of Innocents, which
resounds in the tale, has been amply discussed. 1* Further, St. Nicholas' ties to the Virgin Mary, whose honor is stressed by the Prioress,
imply his presence as well. During some periods in the Middle Ages
St. Nicholas and St. Mary actually vied with one another for popularity,
and they have been considered counterparts of one another: St. Mary
is the heavenly intercessor (cf. B^2 1667-1670), 2* while St. Nicholas
is the earthly 'general helper.' 3* This counterpartite scheme of
homage is present in the Prioress's Tale also.

In the stanza in which the Prioress specifically mentions St. Nicholas
(B^2 1699-1705), she states that the early learning of the widow's little
son is attributable to his character, "For sely child wol alday soone
leere." This precocity, she continues, always reminds her of St.
Nicholas "For he so yong to Crist dide reverence." As is frequently
pointed out, the saint is the patron of schoolboys, and he was, of
course, noted for his diligence to study, even as a child. 4* But that
his precocity should refer specifically to the incident in his legend in
which he is supposed to have abstained from the breast on fast days,
5* as is always pointed out by editors of the tale, is an unnecessary
assumption. The abstention legend is a commonplace event found in
the canons of several saints. 6* A more distinctive legend of St. Nicholas is that in which he is reputed to have stood in his bath for two
hours immediately following his birth. 7* Since graphic representations
of this scene depict the newborn saint with hands clasped in prayer and
eyes heavenward, this can certainly be considered the earliest instance
of piety in Nicholas' life. 8* An allusion to St. Nicholas' fasting at the
breast is more appropriately attributed to a second passage: "But by
the mouth of children thy bountee/ Parfourned is, for on the brest
soukynge/ Somtyme shewen they thyn heriynge" (B^2 1647-1649).

There are other details in the Prioress's story of the murdered
child which suggest the legend of St. Nicholas of Myra. For example,
there is reference to the boy's "body sweete" (B^2 1872) and to his
"tombe of marbul stones cleere" (B^2 1871). While sweetness is surely
not the property of any single saint, the legend of St. Nicholas' Manna,
with its pun on <u>myrrhe</u> and <u>Myre</u> 'Myra' (of which he was bishop), was
famous, 9* and the pilgrimage to his tomb at Bari became well known
because of it. The scent and healing power of the manna were such that
Nicholas was the patron saint of both apothecaries and perfumers. 10*
And the "greyn" (B^2 1852) also is reminiscent of the Nicholas legends,

for spices - this one probably 'grain of paradise' (cardamon) - are mentioned continually as symbols of the saint. 11* What is particularly interesting about the use of "greyn" in the Prioress's Tale is that Chaucer has also used it in connection with another sweet, St. Nicholas-related character in the Miller's Tale. 12*

The saint's connection with the content of the tale is also noteworthy. One of the many legends of St. Nicholas, that of the kidnapped son, appears in several versions, including the Son of Getron (Filius Getronis) and the legend of Basilios (De Basilio). The story is basically as follows:

> During St. Nicholas' celebrations a boy, judged to be seven years old 13* and, sometimes, the only son of a widow, is stolen by heathens and taken to serve their ruler. Even among the heathens the child continues his praise of God and eventually beseeches St. Nicholas for aid. He is returned to his home (in one version, singing), after his mother's piteous lamentations during his absence. 14*

One version has the child rescued from a prison where he has been put following a beating for praising St. Nicholas. 15* And a different, though related, legend of St. Nicholas concerns three sons of a poor, weeping widow, murdered by a son of Satan (whom Joshua Trachtenberg could take for a Jew), 16* who are resuscitated and returned to their mother by St. Nicholas. 17* Concerning the drama Filius Getronis, Karl Young observes the resemblance of the lamenting mother to Rachel and the similarity between the heathen ruler and Herod. 18* Chaucer has made the comparison between the widow and Rachel (B^2 1817) and the heathen kidnappers and Herod (B^2 1764) also.

The legends of St. Nicholas cited above have obvious affinities with the tale told by the Prioress. The main elements of the basic story are comparable to Chaucer's tale of a seven-year-old boy, the only son of a widow, murdered amidst an alien people because of his faith, delivered to eternal life (although in most analogues restored to earthly life) 19* by the Virgin Mary, the object of his particular worship. While I am not suggesting that the Nicholas story is a direct ancestor to the Prioress's Tale, the several versions of the Nicholas legend and the tale do share the same bone structure, showing a family resemblance.

In addition to legends the elements of which are comparable to those of the Prioress's Tale, the St. Nicholas canon includes a number of other stories which concern Jews. The most familiar Nicholas legends concerning Jews are known as "The Image of St. Nicholas" and "The Jew and the Dishonest Christian." In the former story Iconia Sancti Nicolai, a Jew (sometimes generalized as heathen) installs an image of St. Nicholas in his home to protect his possessions when he is away. Thieves rob him and the Jew beats, or threatens to beat, the image, while the saint himself appears to the thieves, telling them to return the Jew's property. The return of his goods results in the Jew's gratitude to Nicholas and conversion to Christianity. 20*

The tale of the Jew and the Dishonest Christian is decidedly more intricate in plot than most of the other legends of Nicholas' canon.

Mary S. Crawford's synopsis of Wace's version is as follows:

> A Christian borrowed money from a Jew, pledging its repayment
> on the image of St. Nicholas. When the money was due, the Christian
> declared that he had paid it. The Jew said that if the Christian would
> swear on the image of St. Nicholas that he had returned the money,
> he would be content. On the appointed day, the Christian enclosed
> the money due in a stick and coming before the image, gave the
> Jew the stick to hold while he took the oath. The Christian then
> taking his stick started on his homeward way. He was run over by
> a cart, the stick was broken, the money fell out, so disclosing the
> fraud. The money was restored to the Jew, the Christian was re-
> vived, and the Jew and all his household were converted to Chris-
> tianity. 21*

The Image of St. Nicholas is a typical conversion story, which might
account for a lenient view toward the Jew, but the Jew and the Dishonest
Christian does not emphasize conversion in any of the versions and
in none is the plot at all dependent on it. While one critic would cite
these legends as evidence that Christians believed the Jews really
admitted the truth of Christianity, and, hence, that the Jews therein
are represented as pious Christians-to-be, rather than as disparaged
Jews, there are numerous stories of Jewish converts who are represented maliciously prior to their change of faith. 22* In the legend
of the Jew and the Dishonest Christian the Jew is represented in his
most contemptible role, the stereotyped moneylender. For this reason
one would expect the attitude of stock medieval repugnance in response
to him at this point in the Nicholas canon. But the Jew is not depicted
as a pariah; he is, in fact, treated sympathetically. The comment on
the Prioress and her tale of full reprisal "by the lawe" is formidable,
therefore.

The affinities of some of St. Nicholas' legends to the Prioress's Tale
and the Jewish overtones of the saint's canon of legends have been
shown. It remains now to examine the implications of the St. Nicholas
references in relation to Chaucer and the Prioress.

There has been much speculation concerning possible anti-Semitism
in the literal level of the tale. Discussion has included the Jews who
are condemned for the murder of the little clergeon, the Little St. Hugh
of Lincoln incident, and the pro- or anti-Semitic feelings of fourteenth
century English society in general. 23* Of particular importance has
been the study by Professor Schoeck. 24*

The reference to St. Nicholas, much like the reference to St. Loy in
the Prioress's description in the General Prologue, serves as a pulse
check for the entire tale. By its very nature, the Nicholas reference
calls for a dualistic examination - 'a look beyond what seems to be to
what is' - for the allusion, like the tale in which it is embedded, is
two-sided. It is on the one hand a benign reference to a kindly patron
of children, Father Christmas; on the other, to the most complex
saint in Christendom, not only the protector of children but the entire
kindergegen 25* (courtship, procreation, childbirth), alleviator of
poverty (even of sexual neediness), 26* patron of sailors, prisoners,

men of all work, and even, it seems, the Jews.

In referring to St. Nicholas directly and in alluding to his legends, Chaucer gives proof of his knowledge of the saint. It cannot be supposed that he knew the legends of St. Nicholas in excised form, that is, that the Jewish aspects were foreign to him. This saint was the most popular in Christendom, and it is said that every English village must have had its St. Nicholas church, for there are over 400 ancient dedications to the saint in medieval England alone, 27* many of which must have included Nicholas representations in sculpture, stained glass or other graphic form. Further, Nicholas' representations were infrequently single scenes, but were more likely to be encountered as series of incidents from his legends or, if single, composites of several legends. 28* And the 527 Latin hymns incorporating his legends would have insured a knowledge of St. Nicholas in the medieval Christian. 29*

That Chaucer knew no Jews, as has been contended, is exactly contrary to possibility; it is highly improbable that he did not know some. First of all, the very occupation of Chaucer's father makes ignorance of Jews remote, for residence in the Vintry would have guaranteed young Chaucer's contact with sailors. 30* Those from Spain, where there had as yet been no expulsion and where Jews had a flourishing late medieval culture, would have been an important source of information. 31* As a child Chaucer may have heard the stories of anti-Jewish atrocities, especially those of the 1349 St. Valentine's Day massacre of Strasbourg and the many others that followed the Black Death all over Europe, since the epidemic was blamed on Jewish well poisoning. 32* Though Chaucer would have been a young child when these events took place, the tales of 1349 were probably long remembered and frequently repeated since the toll in lives was so heavy. Chaucer's own family lost several members in that year. 33*

References to Jews such as those regarding the Black Death may have been unfavorable, and Chaucer would undoubtedly have encountered the "diabolical and grotesque stage-Jew" who lived on in England after the 1290 expulsion. 34* He would have had ample opportunity to compare the mythic Jew with the real-life counterpart, however. Chaucer's early and continuing presence in the royal households would have assured his contact with Jews, and those he met would have been of the highest calibre. In post-expulsion England numerous Jews were summoned to attend the king and members of the royal family and aristocracy. There are records of physicians and other professional Jews who came to England in a steady flow from about 1310 on. 35* There is even a persistent report from reliable sources, Jewish and non-Jewish, that there were enough Jews in fourteenth century England to warrant a post-expulsion expulsion. 36*

Chaucer's contact with Spain would seem to be an especially important source of Jewish knowledge. The record of his presence in Navarre in 1366 is particularly significant. 37* While it is possible that Chaucer was simply passing through on an overland pilgrimage to the shrine of St. James of Compostella, 38* the political involvements of England in Spain at that time make the likelihood remote, or at least secondary. 39* Chaucer's presence in the court of Pedro I of Castile is quite possible. Not only were the Jews still relatively undisturbed in most of Spain, but were especially elevated in Don Pedro's court. Pedro's chief adviser was a Jew, as were numerous other people in high office. 40* Further, it will be recalled, John of Gaunt married Pedro's daughter Constance, to whom Chaucer's wife Philippa became lady-in-waiting. 41* Evidence of these influences on Chaucer is found in his account of the "wikked deeth" of Pedro in the Monk's Tale (B^2 3565-3580).

It is interesting to wonder if Chaucer's contact with Spain also brought contact with Spanish literature, particularly whether he knew the epic El Cid. There is in the poem an episode concerning Jewish moneylenders, Raquel and Vidas, who are deceived in a transaction by the Christian Cid. 42* The episode has affinities with the St. Nicholas legend of the Jew and the Dishonest Christian. As in the saint's legend, the Jews in El Cid are presented without derogatory overtones and as victims of an unjust act (though one critic has excused the Cid's behavior as "an act that may be taken for the vox populi"). 43*

As Raymond Preston has observed, defense of the Prioress's naiveté, in the face of several popes' edicts of toleration, rests on the shakiest of ground. 44* For Chaucer, who was knowledgeable regarding the Jews, to have portrayed her as disregarding church doctrine is incriminating indeed. Nowhere else in the entire canon of his writings does he treat the Jews disrespectfully; only through the mouth of the Prioress do they become "cursed." And that she should be made to refer to St. Nicholas is especially ironic, since he is a saint not of revenge, but of compassion. Though his legends deal with murder - including even the butchering of young boys - he is never vindictive. He never 'blames,' pronounces guilt or levies punishment. He is strong enough to forgive. The Prioress's reference to a saint so completely in opposition to the events in the tale she has piously uttered is a hallmark of Chaucerian irony. That the Jews in the tale were seized and bound (B^2 1810), and, without benefit of hearing, tormented (B^2 1818), sentenced (B^2 1820), drawn by wild horses (B^2 1823), and hung "by the lawe" (B^2 1824) is, indeed, "shameful deeth." The final irony lies in the Prioress's supplication to 'God so merciful,' Pray for us, "we synful folk unstable."

NOTES

1* Marie Hamilton, "Echoes of Childermas in the Tale of the Prioress," Modern Language Review, XXXIV (1939), 1-8.
2* Chaucer citations are from The Works of Geoffrey Chaucer, ed. F. N. Robinson, 2nd ed. (Cambridge, Mass.), unless otherwise indicated.
3* Mary S. Crawford, Life of St. Nicholas (Philadelphia, 1923), p. 12; Adriaan D. DeGroot, Saint Nicholas: A Psychoanalytic Study of His History and Myth (The Hague/Paris, 1965), pp. 161-162.
4* Jacques de Voragine, La Légende Dorée (Paris, 1843), I, 41-47. We are not concerned with the historical facts of St. Nicholas' life - for there is little known about it - but with the legend, i. e., what medieval man knew of Nicholas from art, drama, literature and folklore. See also, Anna B. Jameson, Sacred and Legendary Art, 8th

ed. (London, 1879), II, 451-452; Louis Réau, Iconographie de l'art Chrétien, III Pt. 2 (Paris, 1959), 978.

5* Réau, 976.

6* C. Grant Loomis, White Magic (Cambridge, Mass., 1948), p. 23.

7* Jameson, 461; Réau, 976, 982; Légende Dorée, 41.

8* Jameson, 461; Jules Laroche, Vie de saint Nicolas (Paris, 1886), p. 41.

9* Légende Dorée, 45; Réau, 977, 987-988. See Chapter 5.

10* Emile Mâle, The Gothic Image, tr. Dora Nussey (New York, 1958), p. 329; Laroche, pp. 222ff.

11* DeGroot, pp. 20ff.

12* Discussed fully in Chapter 5.

13* Karl Meisen, Nikolauskult und Nicholausbrauch im Abendlande (Düsseldorf, 1931), discussed by DeGroot, pp. 39-40.

14* DeGroot, pp. 121-122, 39; Jameson, 463-464; Crawford, synopsis of Wace's version, p. 32; Karl Young, The Drama of the Medieval Church (Oxford, 1933), II, 351-360, and Mombritius' Latin text, 492-495.

15* Légende Dorée, 47.

16* Joshua Trachtenberg, The Devil and the Jews (New Haven, 1943), pp. 20-22, 42.

17* Jameson, 454-455, 460.

18* Young, 359.

19* Robinson, p. 734.

19a* For Mombritius' Latin text, see Young, II, 491-492, and 337-351.

20* Réau, 985-986; Légende Dorée, 46; Crawford, p. 31; DeGroot, p. 124; Jameson, 462-463.

21* Crawford, p. 31; Légende Dorée, 45-46; Réau, 986; DeGroot, pp. 119-120.

22* Trachtenberg, for example, pp. 47-50. Note that Jameson, 462, in reporting the legend of the Image of St. Nicholas, calls the Jew parenthetically "an irreverent pagan."

23* Raymond Preston, "Chaucer, His Prioress, The Jews, and Professor Robinson," Notes and Queries, CCVI (1961), 7-8; Cecil Roth, A History of the Jews in England, 2nd ed. (Oxford, 1949); and Florence H. Ridley, The Prioress and the Critics, University of California Publications, English Studies: 30 (Berkeley, 1965).

24* R. J. Schoeck, "Chaucer's Prioress: Mercy and Tender Heart," Bridge, II (1956), 239-255.

25* DeGroot, p. 108.

26* DeGroot, p. 161.

27* Francis Bond, Dedications of English Churches (London, 1914), p. 237; R. L. P. Milburn, Saints and Their Emblems in English Churches (Oxford, 1961), p. 190; Jameson, 451.

28* Réau, 980-988; Jameson, 461.

29* G. M. Dreves and C. Blume, Analecta Hymnica Medii Aevii, 55 vols. (Leipzig, 1886-1922).

30* Chaucer Life-Records, eds. M. M. Crow and C. C. Olson (Austin, 1966), pp. 1-12.

31* Americo Castro, The Structure of Spanish History, tr. Edmund

L. King (Princeton, 1954), pp. 466ff. ; P. E. Russell, <u>The English Intervention in Spain and Portugal in the Time of Edward III and Richard II</u> (Oxford, 1955), pp. 9-10; "Anglo-Castilian trade was important to both countries and merchants and seamen of both countries were well acquainted with each other's ways. Chaucer's shipman naturally knew 'every cryke in Britayne and in Spayne.' Spanish wine from Lepe (near Ayamonte) had, as the Pardoner explained, special qualities which were appreciated - if not approved - in Fleet Street and in Cheapside."

32* Trachtenberg, "The Poisoners," Chap. VII, pp. 97-108.

33* <u>Life-Records</u>, p. 4.

34* Montagu Frank Modder, <u>The Jew in the Literature of England</u> (Philadelphia, 1939), p. 15.

35* Roth, p. 132; Modder, p. 12.

36* Roth, p. 132.

37* <u>Life-Records</u>, pp. 64-65.

38* <u>Life-Records</u>, p. 65.

39* Russell, Chapters I-III; <u>Chaucer's World</u>, comp. Edith Rickert (New York, 1948), p. 325.

40* Castro, p. 471f. ; Russell, p. 21, n. 2.

41* <u>Life-Records</u>, p. 65, n. 2, and Chap. V, pp. 67-93.

42* I am indebted to Prof. Harriet Goldberg, Romance Languages Dept. , Villanova University, for this information.

43* Castro, p. 472, n. 11.

44* Preston, 7.

8

ATTRIBUTES OF ANGER IN THE SUMMONER'S TALE
(ST. THOMAS OF INDIA)

The story told by Chaucer's Summoner on the pilgrimage to Canterbury is a tale full of wrath. The poet has employed ire thematically
and structurally, and wrath afflicts both the main characters in the
tale. But Chaucer has not only used a great quantity of wrath in his
tale; he has something to say of the quality of the sin as well. He de-
votes the main portion of the tale, containing the examination of wrath,
to the friar's pitch to the cantankerous sick man, Thomas, the latter's
refusal to give his worldly goods to the friar's religious house, and
the ultimate bequest. The friar's objective treatment of the rankled
Thomas, calculated to soothe the sick man's ire, builds up to a point
at which the proposals for complete confessional rights and then for
a material gift are openly asked by the friar, and a blunt refusal
promptly shot back by Thomas. It is at this juncture that the two men
change places: the friar loses his shrewd objectivity, and Thomas,
the potential victim, becomes the victimizer of the friar. The friar,
at finding his efforts thwarted, falls prey to the ire which he has
sought to cool in Thomas, and Thomas, in turn, gains mastery over
the friar, reducing the man to the emotional, as well as the physical,
fundament, the rightful abode of friars, as set out in the Dantean prologue. Friar John is ultimately pushed to a state of sputtering, uncon-
trolled anger and a humiliating admission of defeat.

It is significant that the wrath in the Summoner's Tale is embodied
in not one, but in two characters, for Chaucer has made an important
distinction between them; each of the two men is the representative of a
specific type of ire. As the anger is passed from one character to another, its nature changes as well. That Chaucer is exhibiting two distinct kinds of anger is borne out by a reading of his language of attributes, his symbol system which functions as do the marginalia of
medieval manuscripts themselves. To emphasize and contrast the
types of wrath displayed by the friar and the sick man, Chaucer has
presented the attributes in opposing pairs.

Chaucer has used animal imagery in a number of places in the
Summoner's Tale. It is especially noticeable in the description of the
friar's wrath: "The frere up stirte as dooth a wood leoun, " D 2152,
is a standard Chaucerian simile. A few lines later the friar is compared to a wild boar, a simile which is particularly important in this
discussion of wrath, since it is a member of two sets of opposites.
The figure of the wild boar catches the attention first because it echoes
an earlier comparison in the tale, the simile of D 1829, in which the
sick man is described as a domestic boar. His wife complains of his
inactivity, "He groneth lyk oure boor, lith in oure sty. " The prone,

complaining, inactive Thomas and the upright, raging, ferocious
friar are contrasted with different varieties of the same animal figure
in this instance.

A second pair of opposites is the wild boar and the ant (pissemyre),
D 1825, symbols which bookend the main portion of the tale. Through
its associations with ferocity, the wild boar, usually foaming at the
mouth, has been a traditional representative of anger. In classical
literature, Seneca, for example, uses the figure in De Ira: Spumant
apris ora, dentes acuuntur attritu ("Wild boars foam at the mouth and
sharpen their tusks by friction"). 1* Compare Chaucer: "He looked
as it were a wilde boor; / He grynte with his teeth" (D 2160). The
wild boar was eventually adopted in Christian symbolism as the icon
for wrath in the context of the Seven Deadly Sins. 2* The wild boar as
a symbol of ferocity was a medieval commonplace. It could be found
in both secular and ecclesiastical artifacts - stained glass windows,
wall paintings, tapestries, vessels - and in the manuscripts of the
bestiaries. 3* It is used in literature abundantly, Sir Gawain and the
Green Knight being an obvious example, and Chaucer himself has used
the wild boar on many occasions in the Canterbury Tales in connection
with ferocity or specifically with ire. 4*

Although the wild boar is an image which any medieval audience, as
well as contemporary readers, would associate with anger, the symbolism of the pissemyre is more difficult to discover. Chaucer does
not use pissemyre, ampte, or emmet, all M. E. words for 'ant, '
anywhere else in the entire canon of his writing. His choice of the
image is clearly not an offhand one. By combining Thomas' wrath and
the ant in a simile, he makes the connection between the two elements
unambiguous. The wife complains, "He is angry as a pissemyre. "
But what exactly is the quality of an ant's wrath? The most common
reference to the ant is in the words of Solomon: "Go to the ant, thou
sluggard; consider her ways, and be wise" (Prov. 6:6, f.). The ant
is the time-honored symbol of providence, self-reliance, and the
patient acquisition of its necessities by honest labor. The perseverance
of the ant is legendary. A popular illustration of its tenacity is that
of its climbing a hill of sand. The figure is found in a number of medieval literary sources, for example Lydgate's version of Guillaume
de Deguileville's Pilgrimage of the Life of Man (11. 10, 101 ff.). 5*
Furthermore, one of the fables of Aesop, popular in the Middle Ages,
was "The Ant and the Grasshopper, " a tale which emphasizes the ant's
characteristic of providence. In addition to the more common stories
of ants, there was also a tale of gold-guarding ants in medieval currency. It appears in Mandeville's Travels, 6* Vincent de Beauvais'
Speculum naturale (XX, cxxxiv), and Philippe de Thatin's Bestiarie. 7*
In this instance, the ant's strong sense of duty is illustrated. As
guardians of hills of gold, ants can be distracted by only the most
ingenious methods. When they have been successfully tricked, however,
their wrath is boundless.

In an era of black-or-white morality, the ant was presented unequi-
vocally as a symbol of good and would have been recognized as such
by a medieval audience. We are told that the diligence of the tiny "beast"
in providing for itself is so impressive that when the owner of a harvest

sees the ant storing up his grain he "blushes to deny the gleanings of industry to such a thrifty sense of duty. "8* The anger of the pissemyre, therefore, is wrath motivated by infringement on property accrued by honest, painstaking labor. It is the indignation of a just character in the face of unjust action. Chaucer has juxtaposed the ferocious, formidable boar and the tiny, benign ant as symbols of sinful anger and justified anger. The anger of the ant is righteous wrath, wrath emanating from patience.

In De Ira, the source of so many of Chaucer's comments on ire in the Summoner's Tale, Seneca denies the existence of righteous wrath. 9* It was upheld by other classicists, however, and the very fact that Seneca felt compelled to refute the idea, especially that of Aristotle, 10* is proof of its viability in his time. That Chaucer believed in righteous wrath is shown in the Parson's Tale: "Ire is in two maneres; that oon of hem is good, and that oother is wikked" (I 535). The wrath of Thomas, in keeping with Chaucer's belief, is just. Like the provident ant, he has lain up stores of provision with honest labor. (That he has provided well is evidenced by the friar's attraction to his household.) In contrast, the friar's acquisitions have been made by the most despicable route, violation of the confessional. The attempt of Friar John to increase his stores through Thomas has rightly incited the sick man to rage. Nor is Thomas' anger sudden; it has been long accruing; each capon leg has added to the grudge. In this sense, too, it conforms to Chaucer's "goode Ire, " as opposed to "wikked Ire ... that is to seyn, sodeyn Ire or hastif Ire" (I 540). Furthermore, his wife's vulnerability to the friar's wheedling may have initiated a perpetual quarrel in Thomas' household. One can imagine the sick man's reaction to the news that the friar had arrived at his home again.

In an age with an affinity for both strong contrasts and for symmetry, it was natural that the graphic and literary representations of the seven vices should be depicted with their counterbalanced seven virtues. Originating from Prudentius' Psychomachia, the seven contending virtues and vices opposed one another in pairs for mastery over man's soul. This arrangement is the schema of Chaucer's Parson's Tale. Wrath was represented not only by a ferocious, foaming wild boar, as we have seen, but variously as a woman tearing out her hair, a pair of boys wrestling, and frequently by a figure plunging a knife into its breast. 11* Patience, in the pattern of actively opposing vices and virtues, contended with anger. Although in this context patience was not customarily represented by an ant, the ant climbing the hill of sand was, as discussed above, a common figure for patience in the sense of tenacity. Chaucer himself uses the association of sandhills and patience in the Parlement of Foules: "Dame Pacience syttyng there I fond, / With face pale, upon an hil of sond" (PF 242-243.)

While I do not suggest that Chaucer has drawn Thomas the sick man as a figure of simple patience as we know it - the complicated system of subcategories of sins could classify such a seemingly incongruous act as contraception under the larger sin of ire - he has meant to represent the man as diametrically opposite to the friar, a straightforward symbol of wrath. To accomplish this, he has utilized a well-established pair of opposites, a vice opposing its mitigating virtue.

That Chaucer himself connected patience and righteous wrath may be seen in turning again to the Parson's Tale: "This [goode] Ire is with debonairetee, 12* and it is wrooth withouten bitternesse" (I 539).

In addition to animal imagery, Chaucer has used other attributes to indicate that he intended Thomas as a figure of patience exhausted to righteous wrath, as opposed to the sinful wrath of the friar. The very figure of Thomas as a sick man suggests patience: the noun patient 'sick man' is a Middle English derivation from the word patience (OED). The contrast of the prone, inactive Thomas and the physically upright, busy friar is a dramatic one. Spenser seems to extend this idea in the Faerie Queene by representing patience as a physician (I, Canto X, xxiii). Other attributes also suggest the opposition of John and Thomas. In one of Chaucer's very iconographic lines, D 2091, the friar advises Thomas "Hoold nat the devels knyf ay at thyn herte." As mentioned above, one of the most common icons for anger is a figure holding a knife at its breast. This symbol of wrath can be seen, for example, in Lyons Cathedral, in Prudentius' Psychomachia, and at Amiens Cathedral. 13* Preceding the line containing the figure of wrath, and also preceding the exchange of dominant roles in the tale, the friar boasts that Thomas will "me finde as just as is a squyre." The contrast of these two lines is particularly applicable to the juxtaposition of the virtue of patience and the vice of ire. The squyre, '(builder's or carpenter's) square,' even today figuring in expressions of virtue - "a square deal," "to make things square," "to be on the square" - was a medieval image not only for good but, in at least limited use, specifically for patience. Adolf Katzenellenbogen, in discussing a medieval miniature in which ire opposes patience, finds that "Patientia turns away from this wild scene [depicting Ira], holding a set-square." 14*

The two lines, D 2090-2091, suggest more than the opposition of the two men as the vice of wrath and the virtue of patience. If the figures are considered as self-contained, total symbols, rather than as two men with opposing emotions which happen to be symbolized, they constitute another set of contrasts in themselves. The line containing the icon for anger specifies not just a knife, but "the develes knyf." Friars, it will be recalled, were frequently used as symbols for the Devil, 15* whose special sin is ire. 16* Indeed Tertullian, in De Patientia, has represented Patience as a woman opposing a devil who undoubtedly symbolizes anger. 17* The square in D 2090, considered along with lines such as D 1977-1980, outlines Thomas as a total symbol also. The choice of the name Thomas for the sick man who is being urged to contribute money for church building suggests St. Thomas of India. This saint, it will be recalled, is credited not only with the building of churches, but with his disdain for gold. What is particularly telling is that the symbol of St. Thomas was the builder's square, previously mentioned. 18* The friar has asked Thomas for money for church buildings. By contrast, St. Thomas gave money intended for church building to the poor, choosing to construct churches of spiritual materials. Therefore he represents Christian faith. In their roles of St. Thomas and the Devil, the two men in the Summoner's Tale offer a vivid contrast.

It is interesting to speculate that the vita of St. Thomas gives further sentence to the Summoner's Tale. The most widely known legend concerning this saint is that which gave him the "Doubting Thomas" title. The scene in the tale in which the friar is groping in Thomas' garments for the treasure which the sick man has "hyd in pryvetee" (D 2143) strongly suggests an ironic inversion of the biblical incident in which St. Thomas, doubting Christ's presence after the Crucifixion, thrusts his hand into the wounds to allay his faithlessness. 19* This incident was well represented in medieval art and must have been widely known, in part, because it could not be easily confused with incidents from other saints' lives. It can be seen, for example, at Chartres, Semur and Tours. 20* The life of St. Thomas seems to have been quite familiar among the medieval English, judging from ancient church dedications alone. 21* But the handling of Christ's wounds by Thomas would probably have been indelibly impressed on them from another source, the mystery cycle drama. 22* Chaucer confirms the import of the drama in the lives of common men in the Miller's Tale especially. Thomas' doubt represented a conflict between the forces of Christ and the forces of the Devil, a struggle which surely engaged the audience's emotions. Judging by our knowledge of audience involvement in this drama - the actors' speeches to the crowd in the Towneley play of Noah alone will illustrate the point - we can surely assume not only a lasting impression of the St. Thomas story, but a ready recognition of, and response to, a corollary. Medieval appreciation of a serious religious subject turned "up-so-doun" can be gauged by the mock-Nativity in the Second Shepherds' Play, a classic example of such inversion. One can almost hear the hissing and cheering at the triumph of the good guy, St. Thomas, over the wrath-ridden, Devil-like Friar John.

NOTES

1* De Ira (I), in Moral Essays, tr. John W. Basore (London, 1928), I, 108-109.
2* Morton W. Bloomfield, The Seven Deadly Sins (East Lansing, 1952), p. 60.
3* Ibid., pp. 232, 227, etc.
4* KnT, 2070; Mel, 2515-2520; MkT, 3299; Bo. 4, m. 3, 1310-1315; m. 4, 1415-1420; m. 7, 1610-1615; Troilus, 14 times; LGW, 980-1121.
5* Guillaume de Deguileville, Pilgrimage of the Life of Man Englisht by John Lydgate, ed. F. J. Furnivall, EETS e. s. 83, Part II (London, 1901), l. l. 10, 101ff.
6* Mandeville's Travels, ed. Paul Hamelius, EETS 153 (London, 1919 pp. 200-201.
7* Le Bestiaire de Philippe de Thaün, ed. Emmanuel Walberg (Lund, 1900).
8* T. H. White, The Bestiary, A Book of Beasts (New York, 1954), p. 98.
9* De Ira, I, 128-129.
10* Ibid., II, 194ff.

11* E. W. Tristram, English Wall Painting of the Fourteenth Century (London, 1955), p. 105. See also, Emile Mâle, The Gothic Image, tr. Dora Nussey (New York, 1958), p. 113, etc.

12* Debonairetee was found as a sub-category of patience, as a companion of patience as the corrective virtue of wrath, or occasionally, in place of patience.

13* Tristram, p. 105; Mâle, p. 143, fig. 54; p. 124, fig. 68; Adolf Katzenellenbogen, Allegories of the Virtues and Vices in Mediaeval Art, trans. J. P. Crick (New York, 1964), p. 12.

14* Katzenellenbogen, loc. cit.

15* H. S. Bennett, Chaucer and the Fifteenth Century (Oxford, 1961), pp. 24-25.

16* Bloomfield, pp. 131, 190, 214-215.

17* Cap. XV. 4, cited by C. S. Lewis in The Allegory of Love (New York, 1958), p. 64.

18* Francis Bond, Dedications of English Churches (Oxford, 1914), p. 58; the Legenda Aurea; Louis Réau, Iconographie de l'art chrétien (Paris, 1958), III, see Thomas. For the vita, see Butler's Lives of the Saints, eds. H. Thurston and D. Attwater, 4 vols. (New York, 1956); S. Baring-Gould's Lives of the Saints, 2nd ed., 13 vols. (London, 1897).

19* John, 20: 24-29.

20* Mâle, p. 304, n. 2, and Fig. 147.

21* Bond, pp. 330, 56-57.

22* The York cycle contains both "The Incredulity of Thomas" (no. 42) and "The Appearance of Mary to Thomas" (no. 46); the Towneley includes "Thomas of India" (no. 28); and the Coventry "Pilgrim of Emmaus" (no. 38) includes the Doubting Thomas story.

9

ST. SIMON IN THE SUMMONER'S TALE*

Like Alice's rabbit hole, the St. Simon oath in the Summoner's Tale
(D 2094) not only leads us down below the surface, but shows us another stratum of meaning there. The context of the oath is the quarrel
between Friar John and the old, sick Thomas. In addition to his long-
term hospitality, Thomas has been asked to give the conniving friar
confessional rights and money as well. Thomas, who has already explained his exhausted funds (D 1948-1953), is completely irritated
by the friar's continued entreaties and replies adamantly, "Nay, ...
by Seint Symoun!" The friar's request specifically points up con-
fession and mendicancy, respectively "the source of the friars' power
and ... the source of their livelihood and their riches," 1* the two
facets of fraternal activity on which secular attacks were most frequently trained. By violating these two practices, the friar immediately
reveals himself as a false apostle 2* and, hence, a prime target for
Chaucer's satire. It is reasonable to expect, then, that the immediate
answer to the friar's request will take advantage of the opportunity
for satire just presented.
    Reference to lives of saints named Simon yields nothing that could
enhance the satire of the Summoner's Tale. 3* The Simon of D 2094,
therefore, can hardly be a saintly saint; a non-saint is required.
Chaucer's use of "seint" in this instance can certainly be regarded as
ironic, as it is in other instances, such as "Seint Idiot" (Troilus, 1,
910) or, frequently, "Seint Venus" (for example in RR, 5953). Similar
usage is pointed out by Owst, who reminds us of the dignity accorded
"Sir Judas," "Sir Caiaphas" and "Sir Pilate." 4* And Arnold Williams
has discussed the dignified treatment of Pilate in the medieval
drama. 5*
    An oath by a tarnished holy man is appropriate for answering a cor-
rupted friar, and no one could be a more apt reference for the Summoner's friar than the arch-false apostle, Simon Magus. The colorful
story of Simon Magus, the early ancestor of Dr. Faustus, has been widely
disseminated; there are many variations on several points and some
of the material is clearly fanciful. 6* Although much scholarly effort
has been devoted to finding the historical Simon within the legend, we
are not here concerned with separating fact from fiction to arrive at
some ultimate truth. The Simon Magus of popular medieval conception
- the figure found in artifacts and secular literature - is of more value
in this instance. A review of the salient points of the legend may be
helpful.

    The vainglorious Simon Magus, or Simon the Magician, aspiring to

* This chapter has appeared in slightly altered form in Chaucer Review, V (1971), 218-224.

godhead, converted many people to his worship through magic. To further his conversions, he tried to buy from Sts. Peter and John the right of laying on of hands (hence the term simony). As a favorite of Nero, he performed his magic at the Roman court and eventually contested his power there with St. Peter. He was able to temporarily discredit Peter and Paul and was the precipitator of their martyrdom. Ultimately he attempted a flight to heaven from a high tower, was unsuccessful, and crashed to his death on the pavement. 7*

Obviously, then, "St. Simon" is anything but holy. It is interesting, however, that as recently as 1958 Louis Réau included him in the canon of saints in Iconographie de l'art Chrétien, saying, "Bien que ce patron des heretiques soit le contraire d'un saint, il merite, autant que Satan, sa place dans un repertoire de l'iconographie chrétienne." 8* And Simon Magus has, of course, been long in the company of Sts. Peter and Paul, included in their legends in literature, such as the Legenda Aurea and the Apocryphal Acts of the Apostles, and in windows and carvings of medieval cathedrals. 9* Owst has discussed the closeness of stories of saints and devils in the Middle Ages. 10*

Generically, Simon Magus is an antichrist. (The OED refers to "the first Antichrist, Simon Magus.") The points at which the legend coincides with, or is reminiscent of, that of the Antichrist are striking. Since "it is very likely that 'Antichrist' is originally nothing else than the incarnate devil," a human opponent of God, it is not difficult to understand that "the time came when people saw Antichrist, or the fore-runner of Antichrist, in every ecclesiastical, political, national, or social opponent, and the catchword 'Antichrist' sounded on all sides." 11* In medieval usage, 'Simon Magus,' 'antichrist' and 'devil' seem to be put varying degrees of specificity for the same concept. The practice can be seen in William Dunbar's Birth of Antichrist, for example, wherein the three terms are interchangeable. Bousset, in his Antichrist Legend, has adequately explained the overlapping of the three figures. 12* It is safe to assume, then, that Chaucer's Thomas, in invoking Simon Magus, is injecting a specific antichristian figure into an atmosphere already heavy with diabolic implications. This God-emulator - call him an 'antichrist' or 'Simon Magus' - has not the dignity of a Miltonic Satan, or of the devil of the Friar's Tale, for that matter, but rather a pompous, despicable corruptness. He is kin to the devils in the medieval mystery plays who are hissed off the stage after the Last Judgment with the decorum of a Laurel and Hardy exit. While we can admire the Satanic types, who have long since overcome their initial falls from grace, we anticipate the downfalls which the antichrists so richly deserve. Since the summoner of the Friar's Tale is not even the peer of the devil, and inasmuch as the Summoner's Tale is a 'quytyng' of the Friar's Tale, the Summoner's friar could scarcely have been made an almost-admirable devil. He had to be a figure clearly worthy of contempt and deserving a fall.

Friars were not infrequently used as medieval symbols for the devil. 13* The first lines of the prologue to the tale contain the devil-friar equation "Freres and feendes been but lyte asonder" (D 1674). Implicitly the diabolic element of the friar has been present in the tale from its beginning also, since the very theme, ire, was considered the particular province of the devil. 14* It will be recalled that in <u>Piers Plowman</u>, this 'sin of the Devil, ' Ire, <u>is</u> a friar. 15*

There are numerous indications in the Summoner's Tale that Chaucer intended to allude to Friar John as Simon Magus. The friar's request for gold (D 2099), only a few lines after the Simon oath, is reminiscent of Simon Magus' boast "I will exhibit abundance of gold. " 16* A bit further, the friar tells Thomas that unless he saves his religious house with a gift of money "elles moste we oure bookes selle" (D 2108). Simon Magus also referred to the disposal of his books. (He threw his into the sea.) 17*

There is much concerning the diabolic element of the friar, which again, is comparable to the fiendish genealogy of Simon Magus. Concerning Simon, St. Peter said, "There are in this magician two substances, that is of man and of the devil. " 18* And there were many such statements concerning the parentage of Antichrist, whose father was named as "pe devil" or "pe feind of hell."19* Sometimes, however, this half-man, half-devil figure was supposed to have been "begotten by a friar and born of a nun. " 20* This aspect of Friar John is shown, ironically, when he chides Thomas for wrath, saying that it is the work of the devil - "This maketh the feend" (D 1833) - which provoked the sick man. Further, in the tongue-in-cheek condemnation of Thomas made by the lord at the end of the tale, we are told of the bequest: "I trowe the devel putte it in his mynde" (D 2221). And there are icons for the devil's chief sin, anger, such as the bowe (D 2066), arrow (D 2068), and the devil's knife (D 2091), which heighten the diabolic implication. 21* It is also interesting that this tale is set in the middle of the month influenced by Mars, the planet of wrath and of the devil. 22*

In a treatise attributed to Simon Magus, <u>The Great Announcement</u>, in which the magician's teachings were revealed, Simon claimed that fire was the chief element of the universe: "The principle of all things is fire. " 23* There are references to fire in the Summoner's Tale. For example, after the supplications by the friar, Thomas' anger is such that "He wolde that the frere had been on fire, / With his false dissymulacioun" (D 2122-2123). In D 1981-1982 the friar tells Thomas that his wrath is that "With which the devel set youre herte afyre. "

There are in the Summoner's Tale a number of references which, while not necessarily used in precisely corresponding ways, are present, nevertheless, in the antichristian legend. The mention of the serpent (D 1994, 2001), for example, recalls Simon Magus' claim that he could cause brass serpents to move. 24* Peter and Paul (D 1819) are prominent in Simon's legend, as discussed above. Seneca (D 2018) is the teacher of Nero, who, in the <u>Legenda Aurea</u>, figures in some of Simon Magus' sorcery. 25* And Elye (Elias), mentioned in D 2116, is one of the traditional witnesses in the legend of Antichrist. 26* The incident of the dead child (D 1852f.) is reminiscent of one of the best known of Simon Magus' exhibitions. Through his magic, he was able to create the illusion of having resuscitated a dead youth. 27* Friar John, similarly, creates the illusion of having raised the dead child of Thomas from death not to life, but to heaven.

The element of pride is important in the legend of Simon Magus, of course, for it is that sin, the first and greatest and the progenitor of the other sins, which has caused his fall, as it ultimately causes the friar's. Friar John's vainglory shows from the first, with his aspiration to superiority. The Biblical tone of D 1818-1822, with its mention of 'rent' and 'fishing men's souls,' soon turns to irony when contrasted with the friar's claims of eminence, first in contrast to "thise curatz" (D 1816), then in comparison to "burel folk" (D 1870-1876), and finally even relative to other friars (D 1955-1957). He rapidly accumulates the deserts which make a fall mandatory. Ironic predictions of the downfall are hinted in lines such as "An irous man, God sende hym lytel myght!/ It is greet harm and certes greet pitee/ To sette an irous man in heigh degree" (D 2014-2016). The height here is not only applicable to Friar John's pride, but suggests the tower and Simon Magus' loss of might in trying to fly from it, as well. Earlier (D 2009-2010), the friar preaches that "ire engendreth homycide, / Ire is, in sooth, executour of pryde." In D 2008 "it is destruccion." And the friar's simile of D 1938-1939 - "right as an hauk up at a sours/ Up springeth into th'eir" - vividly reminds us of the beginning of Simon Magus' flight toward heaven when the power of his supporting demons has not yet been negated by the might of Christ as exercised by St. Peter. 28* Beatrice Brown has discussed this "leaping up" to God before the "pulling down" by St. Peter. 29*

The Summoner's Tale contains ironic references to the friar's faithfulness, some of which are suggestive of Simon Magus. Thomas asks John to promise that the bequest will be fairly shared: "This shaltou swere on thy professioun, / Withouten fraude or cavillacioun" (D 2135-2136). The friar answers "by my feith" and then accuses Thomas of falseness, though Thomas has given exactly as promised. The irony continues when, under the guise of chastising Thomas, the lord accuses the sick man of the friar's sin of "vanytee, " and calls him "false blasphemour" and "demonyak" (D 2208, 2213, 2240), both terms apt for Simon Magus. The lord's final pronouncement on Thomas is also ironic in that it is so fit for the diabolic John: "Lat hym go honge hymself a devel weye!" (D 2242).

Possibly no other Canterbury tale exceeds the Summoner's Tale in instances of word play. 30* There are the puns such as that on "arsmetrike" (D 2222), and in the line "What is ferthyng worth parted in twelve?" (D 1967). And there is the paronomasia of lines such as D 1916-1917, with its chaced: chaast turn. The lord also seems to be issuing a double entendre in the epilogue, where twice he uses the word savour (D 2196, 2226). In view of the Simon Magus allusion, with its pretentions to the station of Christ, this is possibly a play on the word Saviour, as well as savour 'aroma, essence.' It is also possible that a similar twist is meant in D 2113. Initially, the line seems to substantiate the antichristian character of the friar. If the world does not believe in and support the fraternal orders it faces "destruccioun" (D 2110); the sun will be taken from it. This threat is included in all versions of the legend of Antichrist. ' "To the sun he shall say, Fall, and he falleth, " ' and ' "The sun shall he turn to darkness, and the moon to blood" ' are typical of such prophesies. 31* The line also suggests the Sun of Heaven and the Son of God. The Antichrist of the English play of that name boasts that he sent God's "sonne" to die on the cross, and some twenty-seven lines later, that now he is "goddes sonne." 32* Simon Magus, similarly, claims to be God's son and calls God "my Father." 33* The implications of divinity in 2113, then, seem a distinct possibility.

The most outstanding episode of the legend of Simon Magus and the antichristian stories, and certainly the most significant correspondence with the Summoner's Tale, is the final fall. Each of the main figures ascends to a height reached through his own pride, and, as just reward, each crashes ignominiously to the depths. The human fundament claims Friar John and Simon Magus plummets to the fundament of the court of Rome. And there is a final parallel between the fall in the legendary tradition from which Simon emerges and in the Summoner's Tale. It is supplied by a detail from the play of Antichrist and from an English version of the Simon Magus story. Just after the challenger of God in the play has declared his omnipotence, he falls as a great clap of thunder breaks over his head. 34* Similarly, in the English metrical version, "Simon 'fell and brast insondere / And his saule went to hell wip thondir.' " 35* It is intriguing to wonder if Chaucer thought of this aural detail in connection with the fall of the Summoner's friar, since immediately following the bequest (D 2149) he spends two lines of verse describing the earbreaking cataclysm of the "soun."

NOTES

1* Arnold Williams, "Chaucer and the Friars," Speculum, XXVIII (1953), 505.
2* Ibid., 506f.
3* H. Thurston and D. Attwater, eds., Butler's Lives of the Saints, 4 vols. (New York, 1956); S. Baring-Gould, Lives of the Saints, 2nd ed., 13 vols. (London, 1897).
4* G. R. Owst, Literature and Pulpit in Medieval England (New York, 1961), p. 114.
5* Arnold Williams, The Characterization of Pilate in the Towneley Plays (East Lansing, 1950).
6* G. N. L. Hall, "Simon Magus," Encyclopaedia of Religion and Ethics, ed. James Hastings (New York, 1961), II, 514-525; M. R. James, ed., "Acts of Peter," Apocryphal New Testament, pp. 307-333.
7* Ibid. See also P. M. Palmer and R. P. More, eds., Sources of the Faust Tradition from Simon Magus to Lessing (New York, 1936).
8* Réau (Paris, 1958), III, pt. iii, 1223-1225.
9* Ibid.; Émile Mâle, The Gothic Image, tr. Dora Nussey (New York, 1958), pp. 296-298; Anna Jameson, Sacred and Legendary Art (Boston, 1895), I, 210.
10* Owst, p. 110f.
11* W. Bousset, "Antichrist," Ency. Rel. and Ethics, I, 578, 581; see also Joshua Trachtenberg, The Devil and the Jews (New Haven, 1943), p. 39.
12* London, (1896), pp. 147-150, 180-181.

13* H. S. Bennett, Chaucer and the Fifteenth Century (Oxford, 1961), pp. 24-25.

14* Morton W. Bloomfield, The Seven Deadly Sins (East Lansing, 1952), pp. 131, 190, 214-215.

15* B-text, Passus V, 136.

16* "Recognitions of Clement," The Ante-Nicene Fathers, ed. Alexander Roberts and James Donaldson (Grand Rapids, Mich., 1951), VIII, 99.

17* Palmer and More, p. 36.

18* Ibid., 37-38.

19* R. Morris, ed., Cursor Mundi, EETS 66 (London, 1877), 1260, 1262.

20* Owst, p. 93, n. 6.

21* I have discussed these icons more fully in "Attributes of Anger in the Summoner's Tale," Chapter 8.

22* (D 1782-1783); Bloomfield, pp. 233-234, 437, etc.

23* Hall, 516.

24* Mâle, p. 297.

25* Mâle, p. 296.

26* Bousset, Ant. Leg., p. 203f.; N. B., p. 207.

27* "Acts of Peter," pp. 325-329.

28* Ibid., p. 331.

29* "Marlowe, Faustus, and Simon Magus," PMLA, LIV (1939), 108-109.

30* Paull F. Baum, "Chaucer's Puns," PMLA, LXXI (1956), 225-246, and "Chaucer's Puns: A Supplementary List," PMLA, LXXIII (1958), 167-170; Helge Kökeritz, "Rhetorical Word-Play in Chaucer," PMLA, LXIX (1954), 937-952.

31* Bousset, Ant. Leg., p. 176. I have presented allusions to St. Thomas in the figure of the sick man Thomas in the SumT. (See "Attributes of Anger in the Summoner's Tale," preceding.) Samuel C. Chew has discussed the sun as one of St. Thomas' attributes in later art in The Virtues Reconciled (Toronto, 1947), p. 89 and p. 141, n. 48. It is also interesting that St. Thomas is discussed by St. Augustine in Against Faustus (Legenda Aurea, ed. T. Graesse [Dresden/Leipzig, 1846], Cap. V, p. 33).

32* The Play of Antichrist from the Chester Cycle, ed. W. W. Greg (Oxford, 1935), 11. 486, 514.

33* "Acts of Peter," p. 331.

34* Karl Young, The Drama of the Medieval Church (Oxford, 1933), II, 390.

35* Brown, PMLA, LIV, 97-98, n. 42; see also C. G. Jung, Symbols of Transformation, tr. R. F. C. Hull (New York, 1956), p. 45.

10

THE ST. JOCE OATH IN THE WIFE OF BATH'S PROLOGUE*

The relationship of Alice, Wife of Bath, to her fourth husband was atypical of her marriages in one important aspect: in the fourth instance only there was no significant age difference between the two. It is most ironic that Alice, always inordinately proud of her physical assets, should have had a philandering husband during the period of the fourth marriage, a time when she was in her prime and when the degree of physical attraction between the husband and wife would be expected to be greatest. There is not a more vivid section in the Wife of Bath's Prologue than the one concerning Alice's reactions to this fourth mate, the "revelour" (D 453-502). Enclosed within it is Alice's much-quoted speech on age and the memories of youth (D 469-479), as well as the account of the purgatory-on-earth which the roaming husband suffered for his marital transgressions. It is improbable that any part of such a heightened section should constitute poetic dead weight; every word would surely count. Yet one allusion in this section has been treated phlegmatically.

Alice states, concerning husband Number Four, that she

> ... hadde in herte greet despit
> That he of any oother had delit.
> But he was quit, by God and by Seint Joce!
> I made hym of the same wode a croce.
> (D 481-484)

The use of St. Joce has been attributed to Chaucer's needing a rime for croce. 1* The line following the oath (D 484) is identified as proverbial 2* and explained as meaning "the Wife repaid her husband by making him as angry and jealous as herself." 3* But these explanations do not probe the allusion beyond its surface. Chaucer used St. Joce for a valid reason. There is a much more subtle connection between the proverbial line and the saint than rime.

"The same wode" with which the Wife "quit" her husband would not have been obscure to a fourteenth century audience. The saints were familiar to all strata of medieval society 4* and would have been especially appreciated by a group of religious pilgrims. The identification of an individual saint was accomplished by the use of a symbol representing some aspect of each saint's legend, as we know. The attribute by which St. Joce is identified is a burdoun, a 'wooden shepherd's staff carried by a pilgrim.' 5* In addition to the connotation of 'stick' or 'staff,' however, the word has a second meaning, as shown by research on the pun in A 673 of the Canterbury Tales,

---

* Material in this chapter originally appeared in **Chaucer Review**, I (1966), 85-87.

"[he] bar to hym a stif burdoun, " in which the Pardoner's homosexual
relationship with the Summoner is revealed. Paull F. Baum and D.
Biggins have, with ample literary references, established for burdoun
the double meanings of 'phallus' and '(pilgrim's) staff.' 6* Still greater
weight is given to Chaucer's use of St. Joce for phallic symbolism,
however, by the fact that this saint is frequently represented not only
by a staff, but also by a second symbol, the pilgrim's scrip, as well. 7*
B.D.H. Miller, discussing line A 637, cites the use of burdoun and
escharpe, 'staff' and 'scrip,' as having the extended meanings 'phallus'
and 'scrotum' in the Roman de la Rose. 8* Sidney Heath, describing
the pilgrims' costumes, points out the fact that the burdoun was sometimes decorated with ornamental balls, which would incorporate both
attributes of St. Joce. 9* Paull Baum has also pointed out the double
meanings of 'staff' and 'burden' for croce, 10* making possible the
reading of the line with even further word-play: "I made him of that
burdoun a burden. " And in addition to croce 'burden,' the Middle
English Dictionary shows croce, cros specifically as 'suffering, penance.' 11*

It is also possible that Chaucer thought of further word play on the
noun croce as 'a curved staff,' with the extended meaning of burdoun,
'phallus.' Fourteenth century currency of this meaning is well illustrated by the play on cruz 'cross' and its variants in the Libro de
Buen Amor (c. 1330-1343) by Juan Ruiz, Archpriest of Hita, in the
section of that work entitled "de lo que aconteçió al Arçipreste con
Fernand Garçía, su Menssajero":

115   Mys ojos no verán luz
        pues perdido hé á Cruz
        Cruz, cruzada, panadera
        ....
        fizoş' de la Cruz privado.
        a mí dió rrumiar salvado;
        él comió el pan más duz'.
        ....

121   Quando la Cruz veya, yo siempre me omillava
        santiguávame á ella doquier que la fallava;
        el compaño de çerca en la cruz adorava:
        del mal de la cruzada yo non me rreguardava. 12*

The paronomasia on cruz comes across excellently in the translation
of this section by Elisha K. Kane:
"What Befell the Archpriest through His Messenger Fernando Garcia
[regarding his lady named Cross]"

115   Yes, you'll ne'er behold the light
        Since I've lost my Cross tonight.
        Cross, my Double-Hot-Cross-Bun.
        ....
        Secretly he crossed her though -
        He ate cake while I ate dough -
        She was his delight.
        ....

121   But still whene'er I see my Cross, I bow my
             reverend head
         And bless myself when unawares I chance near
             her to tread,
         What though my pious messenger still takes my
             Cross to bed
         I see no evil in my Cross but worship her
             instead. 13*

And there is the further implication of 'double-crossing, ' also illustrated in this selection from the Libro de Buen Amor, and certainly
possible in the Wife of Bath's Prologue.
    Chaucer's use of the wood of the burdoun for a cross, therefore,
would be most appropriate for a philanderer. Since we are dealing
here not with just any roaming husband, but with a man who has two-
timed Alice, Wife of Bath, the pungency of the allusion is, indeed,
fitting.
    The subtle invocation of St. Joce is brought out not only by line D 484.
There are reminders of the saint in other nearby passages in the Wife
of Bath's Prologue. For example, Alice comments that her husband
was not repaid in kind: "he was quit ... nat of my body" (D 485).
Instead, he suffered public ridicule, after which he, along with every-
one else in the village, was completely deprived of her charms while
she went on a pilgrimage to Jerusalem (D 495). Such a pilgrimage
was the perfect end for a "quitting" that began with Joce, since this
saint was also a patron of pilgrims. 14*
    The Wife of Bath would surely have encountered St. Joce in her
travels, as Winny suggests. 15* She had been to Rome, Santiago in
Spain, Boulogne and Cologne, in addition to three trips to Jerusalem.
The legend of Joce, a seventh century Breton saint, 16* was well
disseminated in Europe. His cult was widespread, radiating from
Ponthieu north into the Netherlands, then into Germany and Alsace
and into Switzerland. There are Swiss, German and French church
dedications to St. Joce, and the iconography of this popular ecclesiastic
extends as far as Innsbruck, where he is represented on the tomb of the
Emperor Maximilian. The name Joce (Josse, Judocus), in its several
forms, was a popular personal one in the Middle Ages and is preserved
in place names as well.17* A festival of St. Joce still survives in this
century. 18*
    St. Joce seems to have been well-known not only in continental
Europe, but in England also. His legend is preserved in several early
English manuscripts. 19* He is especially honored in Winchester, since
his relics are supposed to have been translated to the New Minster
(Hyde) there early in the tenth century. 20* According to tradition,
Charlemagne gave the hermitage of St. Josse-sur-Mer on the coast of
France to Alcuin as a hospice for cross-channel travellers. 21* There
is a record of Charlemagne's having visited the St. Josse abbey in the
ninth century, 22* and in 1377 Chaucer himself was in Montreuil, only
a short distance from St. Josse-sur-Mer. 23*
    It is interesting to wonder if Chaucer also had St. Joce in mind when
he wrote line D 487. Alice states that because of her jealousy and

anger toward her fourth husband "in his owene grece I made hym frye."
It is not only stated that St. Joce was patron de pelerins, but that "on
l'invoquait aussi contre l'incendie" as well. 24*

NOTES

1* Chaucer's Major Poetry, ed. Albert C. Baugh (New York, 1963),
p. 390.
2* B. J. Whiting, Chaucer's Use of Proverbs (Cambridge, Mass. 1934),
p. 181.
3* The Wife of Bath's Prologue and Tale, ed. James Winny (Cambridge,
Eng., 1965), p. 92. W. W. Skeat (ed. The Works of Geoffrey Chaucer,
2nd ed. [Oxford, 1900], V, 303) in his note to D 483-484 cites a
similar passage by Jean de Meung, but the reference is unexplained
in the French also.
4* See Émile Mâle's discussion in The Gothic Image, tr. Dora Nussey,
(New York, 1958).
5* Louis Réau, Iconographie de l'art chrétien, III, pt. 2 (Paris, 1958),
763.
6* Paull F. Baum, "Chaucer's Puns," PMLA, LXXI (1956), 232; D.
Biggins, "Chaucer's General Prologue, A 673," N and Q, n. s. VI
(1959), 435-436.
7* Réau, III, 763.
8* B. D. H. Miller, "Chaucer's General Prologue, A 673: Further
Evidence," N and Q, n. s. VII (1960), 404-406.
9* Pilgrim Life in the Middle Ages (London, 1911), pp. 121-122.
10* Baum, 234.
11* Edited by Hans Kurath and Sherman M. Kuhn (Ann Arbor, 1952),
croce, 2. (a), fig., 1 (c); cros, 1b. (c).
12* Decima edicion, Colleccion Austral, No. 98 (Madrid, 1964), pp.
24-25.
13* The Book of Good Love, 2nd ed. (Chapel Hill, N. C.), p. 24. And
see also A New Pronouncing Dictionary of the Spanish and English
Languages, comp. Mariano Velasquez de la Codena et al. (New York,
1962), Span. cruz, n.; cruzar, v., 1,4; Engl. crotch. Cf. in the
MED, croisin, v., 4 (a) 'to lie across (one another), intersect;'
crossen, v. 'to lie across (something), intersect.' I am indebted to Prof.
E. Carole Brown, of the Department of English, SUNY College/Buffalo,
for the information concerning Juan Ruiz, contained in her forthcoming
article "Juan Ruiz's troba caçurra and the Paronomasial Mode." I
have discussed Chaucer's connection with Spain in the chapter entitled
"St. Nicholas and the Prioress's 'cursed Jewes.' "
14* Réau, III, 763.
15* Winny, p. 92.
16* Butler's Lives of the Saints, eds. H. Thurston and D. Attwater (New
York, 1956), IV, 550.
17* Réau, III, 763; William B. S. Smith, "De la Toponymie Bretonne,"
Language, XVI, no. 2 (1940), 69.
18* Nancy Price, Pagan's Progress: High Days and Holy Days (London,
1954), pp. 117-118.

19* T. D. Hardy, Descriptive Catalogue of Materials Relating to the History of Great Britain and Ireland, Chronicles and Memorials of Great Britain during the Middle Ages (London, 1862), I, 265-269.
20* Liber Vitae: Register and Martyrology of New Minster and Hyde Abbey, Winchester, ed. Walter de Gray Birch (London, 1892), pp. ix, x, 6, 46, 92, 98, 99, 248, 264, 270.
21* Butler's Lives I, IV, 550; Dom Louis Gougnaud, Gaelic Pioneers of Christianity, tr. Victor Collins (Dublin, 1923), p. 79, n. 3; J. Corblet, Hagiographie du Diocese d'Amiens, I (Paris/Amiens, 1868), 74.
22* Corblet, V (1875), 12. See also V, 41ff. for records of St. Joce in old calendars of the church of Amiens, and III (1873), 83-140 for main Joce discussion.
23* Chaucer Life-Records, ed. M. M. Crow and C. C. Olson (Austin, 1966), pp. 49-51.
24* Réau, III, 763.

BIBLIOGRAPHY

Acta Sanctorum [AASS]
"Acts of Peter," M. R. James, ed., Apocryphal New Testament (Oxford, 1924), pp. 307-333.
Aelfric's Lives of Saints, W. W. Skeat, ed., Early English Text Society [EETS] c. s. 76, 82, 94, 114 (London, 1881-1900).
Agnus Castus, A M. E. Herbal, Gösta Brodin, ed., Essays and Studies on English Language and Literature, VI (Cambridge, Mass./Copenhagen, 1950).
Ruth M. Ames, "The Source and Significance of 'The Jew and the Pagan,'" Mediaeval Studies, XIX (1957), 37-47.
Archaeologica Cantiana, Kent Archaeological Society, X (London, 1876).
Sydney Armitage-Smith, John of Gaunt (New York/London, 1905).
Aurora Consurgens, Marie-Louise van Franz, ed., R. F. C. Hull and A. S. B. Glover, tr. (London, 1966).
A. T. Baker, "Saints Lives Written in Anglo-French," Essays by Divers Hands, Transactions of the Royal Society of Literature, n. s. IV (1924), 119-156.
Robert A. Barakat, "Odin: Old Man of The Pardoner's Tale," Southern Folklore Quarterly, XXVIII (1964), 210-215.
Sabine Baring-Gould, Lives of the Saints, 2nd ed. (London, 1897), and rev. ed. (London, 1914), 13 vols.
Ethel R. Barker, Rome of the Pilgrims and Martyrs (London, 1912).
Maurice Bassan, "Chaucer's Cursed Monk, Constantinus Africanus," Mediaeval Studies, XXIV (1962), 127-140.
Paull F. Baum, "The Canon's Yeoman's Tale," Modern Language Notes, XL (1925), 152-154.
——, "Chaucer's Puns," PMLA, LXXI (1956), 225-246.
——, "Chaucer's Puns: A Supplementary List," PMLA, LXXIII (1958), 167-170.
Paul E. Beichner, C. S. C., "Chaucer's Pardoner as Entertainer," Mediaeval Studies, XXV (1963), 160-172.
John B. Bender, Spenser and Literary Pictorialism (Princeton, 1972).
H. S. Bennett, Chaucer and the Fifteenth Century (Oxford, 1961).
Le Bestiaire de Philippe de Thaün, Emmanuel Walberg, ed. (Lund, 1900).
The Bestiary, A Book of Beasts, T. H. White, tr. (New York, 1954).
Bibliotheca Sanctorum, Instituto Giovanni XXIII nella Pontificia università lateranense (Rome, 1961-1968), 12 vols.
D. Biggins, "Chaucer's General Prologue, A 467," Notes and Queries, CCV (1960), 129-130.
——, "Chaucer's General Prologue, A 673," Notes and Queries, n. s. VI (1959), 435-436.

——, "More Chaucerian Ambiguities: A 652, 664, D 1346," Notes and Queries, CCVII (1962), 165-167.

Morton Bloomfield, The Seven Deadly Sins (East Lansing, 1952).

Francis Bond, Dedications of English Churches: Ecclesiastical Symbolism, Saints and Their Emblems (London, 1914).

The Book of Saints, Benedictine Monks, St. Augustine's Abbey, Ramsgate, 4th ed. (New York, 1947).

The Book of Vices and Virtues, W. Nelson Francis, ed., EETS o. s. 217 (London, 1942).

W. Bousset, "Antichrist," Encyclopaedia of Religion and Ethics, ed. James Hastings (New York, 1961), I.

Beverly Boyd, "Chaucer's Prioress: Her Green Gauds," Modern Language Quarterly, XI (1950), 404-416.

Breviarium Ad Usum Insignis Ecclesiae Sarum, Francis Proctor and Christopher Wordsworth, eds., I (Canterbury, 1882).

H. P. Brewster, Saints and Festivals of the Christian Church (New York, 1904).

F. Brittain, Saint Giles (Cambridge, Eng., 1928).

Arthur T. Broes, "Chaucer's Disgruntled Cleric: The Nun's Priest's Tale," PMLA, LXXVIII (1963), 156-162.

Bertrand H. Bronson, In Search of Chaucer (Toronto, 1960).

Beatrice Brown, "Marlowe, Faustus, and Simon Magus," PMLA, LIV (1939), 82-121.

Alban Butler, Lives of the Saints, eds. Herbert Thurston, S. M., and Donald Attwater (New York, 1956), 4 vols.

John R. Byers, Jr., "Harry Bailey's St. Madrian," English Language Notes, IV, 6-9.

Frederick H. Candelaria, "Chaucer's 'Fowle Ok' and The Pardoner's Tale," Modern Language Notes, LXXI (1956), 321-322.

William M. Carroll, Animal Conventions in English Renaissance Non-Religious Prose, 1550-1600 (New York, 1954).

Americo Castro, The Structure of Spanish History, Edmund L. King, tr. (Princeton, 1954).

Ceremonies and Processions of the Cathedral Church of Salisbury, C. Wordsworth, ed. (Cambridge, Eng., 1901).

E. K. Chambers, The Mediaeval Stage (London, 1903), 2 vols.

Chaucer's Major Poetry, A. C. Baugh, ed. (New York, 1963).

Chaucer's Poetry, E. T. Donaldson, ed. (New York, 1958).

Chaucer's World, Edith Rickert, comp., C. C. Olson and Martin M. Crow, eds. (New York, 1948).

Samuel C. Chew, The Virtues Reconciled (Toronto, 1947).

J. E. Cirlot, A Dictionary of Symbols, Jack Sage, tr. (London/New York, 1962).

Thomas B. Clark, "Forehead of Chaucer's Prioress," Philological Quarterly, IX (1930), 312-314.

Rotha Mary Clay, The Mediaeval Hospitals of England (London, 1909).

Ruth Huff Cline, "Four Chaucer Saints," Modern Language Notes, LX (1945), 480-482. [Sts. Frideswide, Cutberd, Yve, Thomas of India].

——, "St. Anne," English Language Notes, II (1964), 87-89.

G. H. Cook, Portrait of Canterbury Cathedral (New York, 1949).

J. Corblet, Hagiographie du diocese d'Amiens (Paris/Amiens, 1868-
    1875), 5 vols.
G. G. Coulton, Art and the Reformation (Oxford, 1928).
M.-J. Couturier, Ste. Bathilde, reine des Francs (Paris, 1909).
Mary S. Crawford, Life of St. Nicholas (Philadelphia, 1923).
M. M. Crow and C. C. Olson, Chaucer Life-Records (Austin, 1966).
W. C. Curry, Chaucer and the Medieval Sciences, 2nd ed. (New York,
    1960).
——, "The Malady of Chaucer's Summoner," Modern Philology, XIX
    (1921-1922), 395-404.
Cursor Mundi, R. Morris, ed., EETS o.s. 57, 59, 62, 66, 68, 99,
    101 (London, 1874-1893).
Ernst R. Curtius, European Literature and the Latin Middle Ages,
    Willard R. Trask, tr. (New York, 1953).
Alfred David, "Criticism and the Old Man in Chaucer's Pardoner's
    Tale," College English, XXVII (1965), 39-44.
H. R. Ellis Davidson, Gods and Myths of Northern Europe (Harmonds-
    worth/Baltimore, 1964).
Arthur de Bles, How to Distinguish the Saints in Art (New York, 1925).
Adriaan D. DeGroot, Saint Nicholas: A Psychoanalytic Study of His
    History and Myth (The Hague/Paris, 1965).
Hippolyte Delehaye, The Legends of the Saints, Donald Attwater, tr.
    (New York, 1962).
Dictionary of Christian Biography, William Smith and Henry Wace,
    eds. (Boston/London, 1877-1887), 4 vols.
A. N. Didron, Christian Iconography, Margaret Stokes, tr., II (London,
    1891).
Myles Dillon, The Cycles of the King (Oxford, 1946).
Gilbert H. Doble, St. Rumon and St. Ronan, Cornish Saints Series, No.
    42 (Shipton-on-Stour, 1939).
E. Talbot Donaldson, Speaking of Chaucer (New York, 1970).
G. M. Dreves and C. Blume, Analecta Hymnica Medii Aevii (Leipzig,
    1886-1922), 55 vols.
Louis Dujardin, Saint Ronan (Brest, 1936).
Agnes B. C. Dunbar, A Dictionary of Saintly Women (London, 1904-
    1905), 2 vols.
T. F. Thiselton Dyer, Folk-Lore of Shakespeare (1883; reis. New
    York, 1966).
Mircea Eliade, Forgerons et Alchimistes (Paris, 1956).
Ralph W. V. Elliott, "Our Host's 'triacle': Some Observations on
    Chaucer's Pardoner's Tale," Review of English Literature, VII
    (1966), 61-73.
English Benedictine Kalendars after A. D. 1100, Francis Wormald, ed.,
    Henry Bradshaw Society vols. LXXVII, LXXXI (London, 1939-1946).
E. P. Evans, Animal Symbolism in Ecclesiastical Architecture (New
    York, 1896).
George Ferguson, Signs and Symbols in Christian Art (New York,
    1966).
Harold Fisch, The Dual Image: The Figure of the Jew in English and
    American Literature (New York, 1971).
John V. Fleming, "The Summoner's Prologue: An Iconographic Ad-
    justment," Chaucer Review, II (1967), 95-107.

78

Brian Foster, "Chaucer's Sëynt Loy: An Anglo-French Pun?," Notes
and Queries, CCXIII (1968), 244-245.
Walter H. Frere, The Kalendar: Studies in Early Roman Liturgy
(London, 1930).
George L. Frost, "That Precious Corpus Madrian," Modern Language
Notes, LVII (1942), 177-179.
Northrop Frye, "Literature and Myth," Relations of Literary Study
(New York, 1967), pp. 27-55.
Thomas J. Garbáty, "The Summoner's Occupational Disease," Medical
History, VII (1963), 348-358.
Alan T. Gaylord, "The Unconquered Tale of the Prioress," Papers of
the Michigan Academy of Science, Arts and Letters, XLVII (1962),
613-636.
Gordon H. Gerould, Chaucerian Essays (New York, 1951).
The Gild of St. Mary Lichfield, F. J. Furnivall, ed., EETS o. s. 114
(London, 1920).
Benjamin L. Gordon, Medieval and Renaissance Medicine (London,
1960).
Louis Gougaud, Gaelic Pioneers of Christianity, Victor Collins, tr.
(Dublin, 1923).
——, Les saints irlandais hors d'Irland (Louvain, 1936).
Robert Graves, The White Goddess (New York, 1948).
Stanley B. Greenfield, A Critical History of Old English Literature
(New York, 1965).
Fernand Gregoronius, History of the City of Rome in the Middle Ages,
Annie Hamilton, tr., 4th ed. (London, 1884).
Joseph E. Grennen, "The Canon's Yeoman and the Cosmic Furnace:
Language and Meaning in the Canon's Yeoman's Tale," Criticism,
IV (1962), 225-240.
Maud Grieve, A Modern Herbal (repr. 1931 ed: New York, 1959),
2 vols.
Philip Griffith, "Chaucer's Merchant's Tale," Explicator, XVI (1957),
Item 13. [St. Damian]
Guillaume de Berneville, La vie de saint Gilles, G. Paris, ed., So-
ciété des anciens textes français, I (Paris, 1881).
Guillaume de Deguileville, The Pilgrimage of the Life of Man, Englisht
by John Lydgate, F. J. Furnivall, ed., EETS e. s. 83, Part II
(London, 1901).
F. W. Hackwood, Inns, Ales and Drinking Customs of Old England
(New York, n. d.).
Jean Hagstrum, The Sister Arts (Chicago, 1958).
G. N. L. Hall, "Simon Magus," Encyclopaedia of Religion and Ethics,
James Hastings, ed. (New York, 1961), II, 514-525.
Marie Hamilton, "Echoes of Childermas in the Tale of the Prioress,"
Modern Language Review, XXXIV (1939), 1-8.
Eleanor P. Hammond, "Two Chaucer Cruces," Modern Language Notes,
XXII (1907), 51-52. [St. Loy]
W. C. Hazlitt, Faiths and Folklore of the British Isles (repr. 1905 ed.:
New York, 1965).
Sidney Heath, Pilgrim Life in the Middle Ages (London, 1911).
Samuel B. Hemingway, "The Two St. Pauls," Modern Language Notes,

XXXII (1917), 57-58.

Laura A. Hibbard, "Chaucer's 'Shapen was my Sherte,'" Philological Quarterly, I (1922), 222-225.

Constance Hieatt, "Oaths in the Friar's Tale," Notes and Queries, CCV (1960), 5-6. [Sts. James, Anne]

Norman D. Hinton, "More Puns in Chaucer," American Notes and Queries, II (1964), 115-116.

F. G. Holweck, A Biographical Dictionary of the Saints (London/St. Louis, 1924).

Edelhard L. Hummel, The Concept of Martyrdom According to St. Cyprian of Carthage (Washington, D. C., 1946).

Arthur R. Huseboe, "Chaucerian Puns on 'Brotel,'" North Dakota Quarterly, XXXI (1963), 35-37.

Arthur Hussey, Testamenta Cantiana: A Series of Extracts from Fifteenth and Sixteenth Century Wills Relating to Church Building and Topography, Kent Archaeological Society, Extra Vol. (London, 1907).

Maurice Hussey, Chaucer's World: A Pictorial Companion (Cambridge, Eng., 1967).

Serge Hutin, A History of Alchemy, Tamara Alferoff, tr. (New York, 1962).

Jacobus de Voragine, The Golden Legend, Helmut Ripperger and Granger Ryan, tr. (New York, 1941), 2 vols.

——, Legenda Aurea, J. G. Theodor Graesse, ed. (Dresden, 1846).

——, La légende dorée (Paris, 1843), 2 vols.

E. O. James, Seasonal Feasts and Festivals (New York, 1961).

Anna B. Jameson, Legends of the Madonna, 2nd ed. (Boston, 1857; corr. ed. London, 1907).

——, Legends of the Monastic Orders (New York, 1901).

——, Sacred and Legendary Art, 8th ed. (London, 1879), II.

C. G. Jung, Psychology and Alchemy, R. F. C. Hull, tr. (New York, 1953).

——, Symbols of Transformation, R. F. C. Hull, tr. (New York, 1956).

Jean A. A. Jusserand, English Wayfaring Life in the Middle Ages, 4th ed. (London/New York, 1950).

R. B. Kaske, "Summoner's Garleek, Oynons, and eek Lekes," Modern Language Notes, LXXIV (1959), 481-484.

Adolf Katzenellenbogen, Allegories of the Virtues and Vices in Medieval Art (New York, 1964).

K. A. Heinrich Kellner, Heortology (London, 1908).

Archdale A. King, Liturgies of the Past (Milwaukee, 1958).

G. L. Kittredge, Chaucer and His Poetry (Cambridge, Mass., 1915).

M. D. Knowles, The Monastic Orders, 2nd ed. (Cambridge, Eng., 1963).

Helge Kökeritz, "Rhetorical Word-Play in Chaucer," PMLA, LXIX (1954), 937-952.

Alice F. Kornbluth, "Another Chaucer Pun," Notes and Queries, VI (1959), 243.

Karl Künstle, Ikonographie der heiligen (Freiburg-im-Breisgau, 1926).

Margaret W. Labarge, Saint Louis (Boston, 1968).

René Largillere, Les saints et l'organization chrétienne primitive

dans l'Armorique bretonne (Rennes, 1925).
Jules Laroche, Vie de Saint Nicolas (Paris, 1886).
Arthur F. Leach, "The Schoolboys' Feast, " Fortnightly Review, LIX,
    n. s. (Jan., 1896), 128-141.
Anatole le Braz, The Land of Pardons, Frances M. Gostling, tr.
    (New York, 1906).
——, La légende de mort. (Paris, 1922).
Albert le Grand, Les vies des saints de la Bretagne Armorique
    (Quimper, 1901).
C. S. Lewis, The Allegory of Love (New York, 1958).
Lucien Lheureux, Bretagne (Paris, 1920).
The 'Liber de Diversis Medicinis', M. S. Ogden, ed. EETS o. s. 207
    (London, 1938).
Liber Vitae: Register and Martyrology of New Minster and Hyde Abbey,
    Winchester, Walter de Gray Birch, ed. (London, 1892).
Lives of Women Saints, C. Horstmann, ed., EETS o. s. 86 (London,
    1886).
C. Grant Loomis, White Magic (Cambridge, Mass., 1948).
R. S. Loomis, A Mirror of Chaucer's World (Princeton, 1965).
John Lowe, "Comments on the History of Leprosy, " Indian Medical
    Gazette, XXXIII (1942), 680-685.
John L. Lowes, "The Prioress's Oath, " Romanic Review, V (1914),
    368-385.
James Lynch, "The Prioress' Gems, " Modern Language Notes, LVII
    (1942), 440-441.
Angus MacDonald, "Absolon and St. Neot, " Neophilologus, XLVIII
    (1964), 235-237.
Magnus MacLean, The Literature of the Celts (Glasgow/Dublin, 1906).
Katherine S. Macquoid, Through Brittany (London, c. 1880).
Francis P. Magoun, Jr., A Chaucer Gazeteer (Chicago, 1961).
Emile Mâle, Religious Art in France in the Thirteenth Century, tr. Dora
    Nussey, 3rd. ed. (New York/London, 1913).
——, The Gothic Image, tr. by Dora Nussey from the 3rd. French edition
    (New York, 1958).
Edward Malone, The Plays and Poems of William Shakespeare (London,
    1821; reis. New York, 1966), XVII.
Kemp Malone, "Harry Bailey and Godelief, " English Studies, XXXI
    (1950), 209-215.
John M. Manly and Edith Rickert, The Text of the Canterbury Tales
    (Chicago, 1940), 8 vols.
The Martiloge, Francis Proctor and E. S. Dewick, eds. (London, 1893).
Sister Mary Immaculate, C. S. C., "Fiends as "Servant Unto Man" in
    the Friar's Tale, " Philological Quarterly, XXI (1942), 240-244.
    [St. Dunstan]
Henry P. Maskell and Edward W. Gregory, Old Country Inns of Eng-
    land (Boston, 1911).
Karl Meisen, Nikolauskult und Nicholausbrauch im Abendlande
    (Düsseldorf, 1939).
Lucy Menzies, The Saints in Italy (London, 1924).
Meurisset, Vie de Ste. Bathilde, reine de France (Lille, 1895).
R. L. P. Milburn, Saints and Their Emblems in English Churches
    (Oxford, 1961).
B. D. H. Miller, "Chaucer's General Prologue, A 673: Further Evi-

dence, " Notes and Queries, n. s. VII (1960), 404-406.

Robert P. Miller, "Chaucer's Pardoner, the Scriptural Eunuch, and the Pardoner's Tale, " Speculum, XXX (1955), 180-199.

Montagu Frank Modder, The Jew in the Literature of England (Philadelphia, 1939).

Allardyce Nicoll, World Drama (New York, 1949).

Dorothy Norris, "Harry Bailey's 'Corpus Madrian, ' " Modern Language Notes, XLVIII (1939), 146-148.

Amy Oakley, Enchanted Brittany (New York, 1930).

Oeuvres de Froissart, Kervyn de Lettenhove, ed. (Brussels, 1869), III.

Old English Martyrology, George Herzfeld, ed., EETS o. s. 116 (London, 1900).

G. R. Owst, Literature and Pulpit in Medieval England (New York, 1961).

Oxford Dictionary of the Christian Church, F. L. Cross, ed. (London, 1957).

George Pace, "The Scorpion of Chaucer's Merchant's Tale, " Modern Language Quarterly, XXVI (1965), 369-374.

Erwin Panofsky, Studies in Iconology (New York, 1962).

The Play of Antichrist from the Chester Cycle, W. W. Greg, ed. (Oxford, 1935).

Austin L. Poole, ed., Medieval England, rev. ed. (Oxford, 1958), 2 vols.

W. E. Post, Saints, Signs and Symbols (London, 1964).

Raymond Preston, "Chaucer, His Prioress, The Jews, and Professor Robinson, " Notes and Queries, CCVI (1961), 7-8.

Nancy Price, Pagan's Progress: High Days and Holy Days (London, 1954).

John Read, The Alchemist in Life, Literature and Art (London, 1947).

Louis Réau, Iconographie de l'art chrétien, Vols. II and III (Paris, 1956-1959).

"Recognitions of Clement, " The Ante-Nicene Fathers, Alexander Roberts and James Donaldson (Grand Rapids, 1951), VIII, 75-211.

Edmund Reiss, "The Symbolic Surface of the Canterbury Tales: The Monk's Portrait, " Chaucer Review, II (1968), 254-272; III (1969), 12-28.

E. Rembry, Saint Gilles, sa vie ... (Bruges, 1882).

Edith Rickert, "Goode Lief, My Wyf, " Modern Philology, XXV (1927), 79-82.

Florence H. Ridley, The Prioress and the Critics, University of California Publications, English Studies: 30 (Berkeley, 1965).

D. W. Robertson, Jr., Chaucer's London (London, 1968).

——, A Preface to Chaucer (Princeton, 1962).

Helen Roeder, Saints and Their Attributes (Chicago, 1956).

Bruce Rosenberg, "The Contrary Tales of the Second Nun and the Canon's Yeoman, " Chaucer Review, II (1968), 278-291.

Cecil Roth, A History of the Jews in England, 2nd ed. (Oxford, 1949).

Beryl Rowland, "Animal Imagery and the Pardoner's Abnormality, " Neophilologus, XLVIII (1964), 56-60.

——, "Chaucer's "Bukke and Hare" (Thop, VII, 756), " English Language Notes, II (1964), 6-8.

Paul G. Ruggiers, The Art of the Canterbury Tales (Madison/Milwaukee, 1965).

P. E. Russell, The English Intervention in Spain and Portugal in the Time of Edward III and Richard II (Oxford, 1955).

Juan Ruiz, The Book of Good Love, Elisha Kent Kane, tr. (Chapel Hill, 1968).

——, The Book of Good Love, Rigo Mignani and Mario A. DiCesare, tr. (Albany, 1970).

——, Libro de Buen Amor, Decima edicion, Colleccion Austral, No. 98 (Madrid, 1964).

Philip Schmidt, "Reexamination of Chaucer's Old Man of the Pardoner's Tale," Southern Folklore Quarterly, XXX (1966), 249-255.

R. J. Schoeck, "Chaucer's Prioress: Mercy and Tender Heart," Bridge, II (1956), 239-255.

Ethel Seaton, " 'Goode lief my wife,' " Modern Language Review, XLI (1946), 196-202.

Paul-Yves Sébillot, Le folklore de la Bretagne, II (Paris, 1968).

James Sledd, "Canterbury Tales, C 310, 320: 'By Seint Ronyan,' " Mediaeval Studies, XIII (1951), 226-233.

Sources of the Faust Tradition from Simon Magus to Lessing, P. M. Palmer and R. P. More, eds. (New York, 1936).

South English Legendary, Charlotte D'Evelyn and Anna J. Mill, eds., EETS o. s. 235, 236, 244 (London, 1956-1959).

Dorothy G. Spicer, Yearbook of English Festivals (New York, 1954).

Herbert W. Starr, "Oaths in Chaucer's Poems," West Virginia University Philological Papers, IV (1943), 44-63.

John M. Steadman, " 'Hir Gretteste Ooth': The Prioress, St. Eligius, and St. Godebertha," Neophilologus, XLIII (1959), 49-57.

Joseph Szövérffy, "Chaucer's Friar and St. Nicholas (Prologue 212)," Notes and Queries, CCXIV (1969), 166-167.

John S. P. Tatlock, "Puns in Chaucer," Flügel Memorial Volume (Stanford, 1916), pp. 228-232.

——, The Scene of the Franklin's Tale Visited, Chaucer Society, 2nd Series, no. 51 (London, 1914).

A. Thomas, S. Ronan et la Tromenie (n. p., 1893).

Joshua Trachtenberg, The Devil and the Jews (New Haven, 1943).

E. W. Tristram, English Wall-Painting of the Fourteenth Century (London, 1955).

Frederick Tupper, "Chaucer's Sins and Sinners," Journal of English and Germanic Philology, XV (1916), 56-106.

——, "The Pardoner's Tavern," Journal of English and Germanic Philology, XIII (1914), 553-565.

——, "Seint Venus and the Canterbury Pilgrims," Nation, XCVII (Oct. 16, 1913), 354-356.

Thomas A. Van, "Second Meanings in Chaucer's Knight's Tale," Chaucer Review, III (1969), 69-76.

La vie de Saint Nicolas par Wace ..., Einar Ronsjö, ed. (Lund, 1942).

Maurice Vloberg, Les fêtes de France (Grenoble/Paris, 1942).

Benjamin B. Wainwright, "Chaucer's Prioress Again: An Interpretative Note," Modern Language Notes, XLVIII (1933), 34-37.

J. Charles Wall, Shrines of British Saints (London, 1905).

F. R. Webber, Church Symbolism (Cleveland, 1938).

Clarence L. Wentworth, "The Prioress' Oath," Romanic Review,
XXVII (1936), 268-269.

Siegfried Wenzel, "Two Notes on Chaucer and Grosseteste," Notes
and Queries, CCXV (1970), 449-451. [St. Peter's sister, A 3485,
and Thomas's insensitivity, D 1825 ff.]

Francis X. Weiser, Handbook of Christian Feasts and Customs (New
York, 1952).

Henry B. Wheatley, The Story of London (London, 1904).

John Whitaker, The Ancient Cathedral of Cornwall, II (London, 1804).

Helen C. White, Tudor Books of Saints and Martyrs (Madison, 1963).

B. J. Whiting, Chaucer's Use of Proverbs (Cambridge, Mass., 1934).

The Wife of Bath's Prologue and Tale, James Winny, ed. (Cambridge,
Eng., 1965).

Arnold Williams, The Characterization of Pilate in the Towneley
Plays (East Lansing, 1950).

——, "Chaucer and the Friars," Speculum, XXVIII (1953), 499-513.

William S. Wilson, "Days and Months in Chaucer's Poems," American
Notes and Queries, IV (1966), 83-84.

Otto Wimmer, Handbuch der Namen und Heiligen (Innsbruck/Wien/
München, 1953).

The Works of Geoffrey Chaucer, F. N. Robinson, ed., 2nd ed. (Boston,
1957).

A. R. Wright, British Calendar Customs, T. E. Lones, ed., Publications of the Folk-Lore Society, Vols. XCVII, CII, CVI (Lon-
don/Glasgow, 1936-1940).

Karl Young, The Drama of the Medieval Church (Oxford, 1933),
2 vols.

Studies in English Literature

Dfl.

13. SCHULZE, Earl J.: Shelley's Theory of Poetry: A Reappraisal.   42,-
36. STONE, Robert K.: Middle English Prose Style: Margery Kempe and Julian of Norwich.   38,-
39. YELTON, Donald C.: Mimesis and Metaphor: An Inquiry into the Genesis and Scope of Conrad's Symbolic Imagery.   46,-
45. ENSCOE, Gerald: Eros and the Romantics: Sexual Love as a Theme in Coleridge, Shelley and Keats.   35,-
49. HOFFMAN, Stanton De Voren: Comedy and Form in the Fiction of Joseph Conrad.   30,-
50. MURRAY, Peter B.: A Study of John Webster.   48,-
51. MULDROW, George M.: Milton and the Drama of the Soul: A Study of the Theme of the Restoration of Men in Milton's Later Poetry.   44,-
57. WEIDHORN, Manfred: Dreams in Seventeenth-Century English Literature.   27,-
58. RICHARDSON, Janette: Blameth Not Me: A Study of Imagery in Chaucer's Fabliaux.   36,-
61. SEAMAN, John H.: The Moral Paradox of 'Paradise Lost'.   26,-
63. MEHOKE, James S.: Robert Graves: Peace-Weaver.   42,-
64. TRACI, Philip J.: The Love Play of Antony and Cleopatra: A Critical Study of Shakespeare's Play.   32,-
66. CHARD, L. F.: Dissenting Republican: Wordsworth's Early Life and Thought in their Political Context.   48,-
67. BURDETTE, Robert K.: The Saga of Prayer: The Poetry of Dylan Thomas.   35,-
68. LYONS, Charles R.: Shakespeare and the Ambiguity of Love's Triumph.   40,-
70. BLUESTONE, Max: From Story to Stage: The Dramatic Adaptation of Prose Fiction in the Period of Shakespeare and his Contemporaries.   52,-
71. WILSON, James H.: Christian Theology and Old English Poetry.   38,-
72. PLOTKIN, Frederick: Milton's Inward Jerusalem: *Paradise Lost* and the Ways of Knowing.   34,-
73. FRAZIER, Harriet C.: A Babble of Ancestral Voices: Shakespeare, Cervantes, and Theobald.   44,-
74. CHERNISS, Michael D.: Ingeld and Christ: Heroic Concepts and Values in Old English Christian Poetry.   55,-
76. DICK, Aliki Lafkidou: Paedeia Through Laughter: Jonson's Aristophanic Appeal to Human Intelligence.   32,-

Studies in English Literature   Dfl.

77. JENKINS, R. B.: Milton and the Theme of Fame.   18,-
78. ROBBINS, Larry M.: Thomas Dekker's *A Knights Conjuring* (1607): A Critical Edition.   48,-
79. DULS, Louisa DeSaussure: Richard II in the Early Chronicles.   46,-
80. DUSSINGER, John A.: The Discourse of the Mind in Eighteenth-Century Fiction.   38,-
81. ELLIS, Herbert A.: Shakespeare's Lusty Punning in *Love's Labour Lost*. With Contemporary Analogues.   44,-
83. CHADWICK, W. R.: The Four Plays of William Wycherley: A Study in the Development of a Dramatist.   48,-
84. MARTIN, Richard: The Love that Failed: Ideal and Reality in the Writings of E. M. Forster.   36,-
85. KAULA, David: Shakespeare and the Archpriest Controversy: A Study of Some New Sources.   36,-
86. CANNON, Charles Dale: A Warning for Fair Women: A Critical Edition.   52,-
88. SIMMONS, James C.: The Novelist as Historian: Essays on the Victorian Historical Novel.   18,-
89. MESSMANN, Frank J.: Richard Payne Knight: The Twilight of Virtuosity.   36,-
91. PRICE, George R.: Thomas Middleton: *Michaelmas Term* and *A Trick to Catch the Old One*. A Critical Edition.   58,-
92. GARDNER, Delbert R.: An "Idle Singer" and his Audience: A Study of William Morris's Poetic Reputation in England, 1858-1900.   30,-
93. GODSHALK, William L.: The Marlovian World Picture.   48,-
94. JACOBUS, Lee A.: Sudden Apprehension: Aspects of Knowledge in *Paradise Lost*.   58,-
95. FREY, David L.: The First Tetralogy Shakespeare's Scrutiny of the Tudor Myth. A Dramatic Exploration of Divine Providence.   42,-
96. HISSIGER, P. F.: *Le Morte Arthur*: A Critical Edition.   38,-
97. COHEN, Kitty: The Throne and the Chariot: Studies in Milton's Hebraism.   44,-
98. BERKOBEN, L. D.: Coleridge's Decline as a Poet.   36,-
99. BALBERT, Peter: D. H. Lawrence and the Psychology of Rhythm: The Meaning of Form in *The Rainbow*.   26,-
100. NATHAN, Norman: Prince William B.: The Philosophical Conceptions of William Blake.   36,-

Studies in English Literature

		Dfl.
101.	BURKHART, Robert E.: Shakespeare's Bad Quartos: Deliberate Abridgments Designed for Performance by a Reduced Cast.	36,-
102.	STELZIG, Eugene L.: All Shades of Consciousness: Wordsworth's Poetry and the Self in Time.	49,-
103.	YOUNG, Art: Shelley and Nonviolence.	38,-
105.	SHANKER, Sidney: Shakespeare and the Uses of Ideology.	44,-
106.	GOING, William T.: Scanty Plot of Ground: Studies in the Victorian Sonnet.	39,-
110.	GARDINER, Judith K.: Craftsmanship in Context: The Development of Ben Jonson's Poetry.	28,-

Studies in American Literature

8.	LONG, Chester C.: The Role of Nemesis in the Structure of Selected Plays by Eugene O'Neill.	44,-
11.	MARKS, Lester Jay: Thematic Design in the Novels of John Steinbeck.	34,-
13.	DUCHARME, Robert: Art and Idea in the Novels of Bernard Malamud: Toward the Fixer.	26,-
14.	PETERSON, Richard K.: Hemingway: Direct and Oblique.	39,-
22.	SPATZ, Jonas: Hollywood in Fiction: Some Versions of the American Myth.	34,-
24.	RICHARDS, Marion K.: Ellen Glasgow's Development as a Novelist.	39,-
28.	SNYDER, John: The Dear Love of Man: Tragic and Lyric Communion in Walt Whitman.	44,-
29.	LAHOOD, Marvin J.: Conrad Richter's America.	28,-
30.	RHODE, Robert D.: Setting in the American Short Story of Local Color, 1865-1900.	38,-

WINTER
SOULSTICE

OTHER BOOKS BY JOHN KILLINGER

The Devil & Harry Potter: A Christian Minister's Defense of the Beloved Novels (St. Martin's, 2002)

Ten Things I Learned Wrong from a Conservative Church (Crossroad, 2002)

Lost in Wonder, Love, and Praise: Prayers and Affirmations for Christian Worship (Abingdon, 2001)

Preaching the New Millennium (Abingdon, 1999)

Raising Your Spiritual Awareness Through 365 Simple Gifts from God (Abingdon, 1998)

The Night Jessie Sang at the Opry (Angel Books, 1996)

Preaching to a Church in Crisis: A Homiletic for the Last Days of the Mainline Church (CSS, 1996)

Day by Day with Jesus: A Devotional Commentary on the Four Gospels (Abingdon, 1994)

Jessie: A Novel (McCracken, 1993)

Beginning Prayer (Upper Room, 1993)

Letting God Bless You: The Beatitudes for Today (Abingdon, 1992)

You Are What You Believe: The Apostles' Creed for Today (Abingdon, 1990)

Christmas Spoken Here (Broadman, 1989)

To My People with Love: The Ten Commandments for Today (Abingdon, 1988)

The God Named Hallowed: The Lord's Prayer for Today (Abingdon, 1987)

Christ and the Seasons of Marriage (Broadman, 1987)

Parables for Christmas (Abingdon, 1985)

Fundamentals of Preaching (Fortress, 1985; SCM, 1986; rev. 1998)

Christ in the Seasons of Ministry (Word, 1983)

The Loneliness of Children (Vanguard, 1980; Editions Robert Laffont, 1983)

His Power in You (Doubleday, 1978)

A Sense of His Presence (Doubleday, 1977)

Bread for the Wilderness, Wine for the Journey (Word, 1976)

The Salvation Tree (Harper & Row, 1973)

World in Collapse: The Vision of Absurd Drama (Dell, 1973)

The Fragile Presence: Transcendence in Contemporary Literature (Fortress, 1973)

Leave It to the Spirit: Freedom and Responsibility in the New Liturgies (Harper & Row, 1971)

For God's Sake, Be Human (Word, 1970)

The Failure of Theology in Modern Literature (Abingdon, 1965)

Hemingway and the Dead Gods (University Press of Kentucky, 1960; Citadel, 1965)